MY FIRST COLORING BOOK!

AS A VIDEO GAME ARTIST AND ANIMATOR I GET TO DESIGN MONSTERS AND CHARACTERS OF ALL SHAPES AND SIZES FOR ALL KINDS OF GAMES.

FOR THE FIRST TIME I WANT TO SEE WHAT SOMEONE ELSE WOULD DO WITH MY SKETCHES AND LINEART.

THANK YOU FOR BUYING THIS COLORING BOOK AND HAVE FUN!

– TOMISLAV

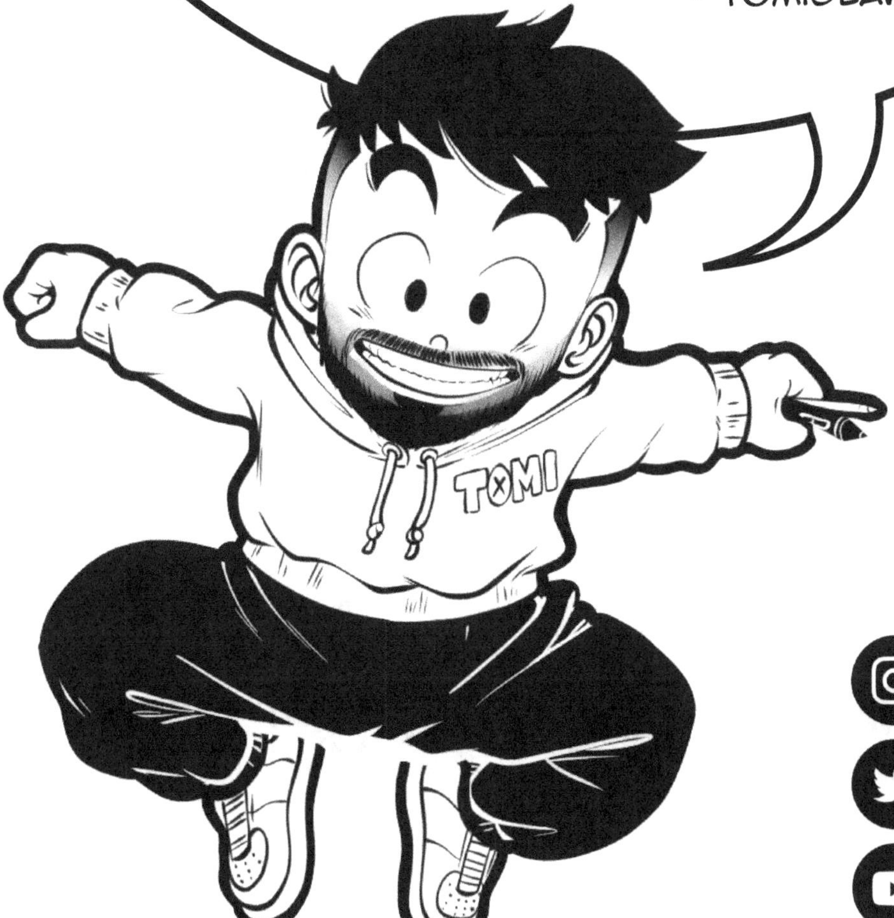

jtomislav

tomislavartz

TomislavArtz

© 2021 Tomislav Jurić

FOR THE BEST CREATIVE EXPERIENCE:

- ADD YOUR OWN TEXT AND DRAWINGS!

- COLOR THEM ANY WAY YOU WANT!

- GIVE THEM NAMES, STRENGHTS & WEAKNESSES!

DON'T BE AFRAID TO BE CREATIVE. NO MATTER HOW 'BAD' YOU ARE AT DRAWING.

THIS IS YOUR CHANCE TO IMPROVE YOUR SKILLS WHILE HAVING FUN AT THE SAME TIME!

E-MAIL ME YOUR CRAZY MONSTERS AND IDEAS FOR NEW MONSTERS AT:

TOMISLAVARTZ+BOOK@GMAIL.COM

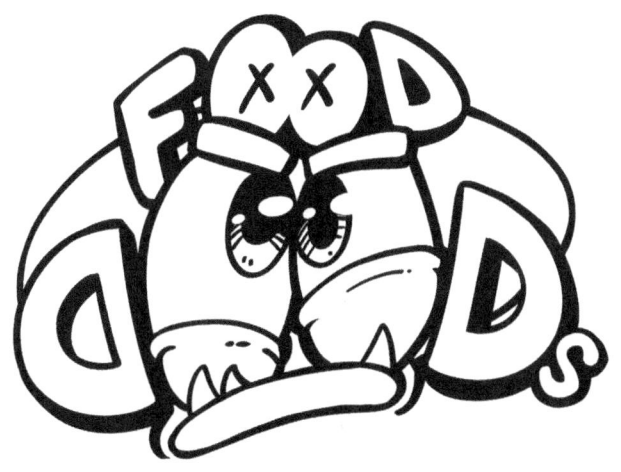

THIS BOOK BELONGS TO:

_____

IF I WERE A MONSTER I'D BE

_____

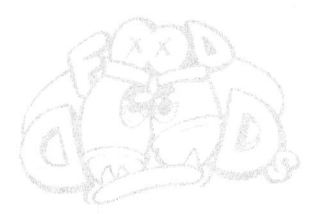

DETAIL LEVEL: HIGH

DIFFICULTY: MEDIUM

SPECIES: BURGER

NAME:

STRENGTH:

WEAKNESS:

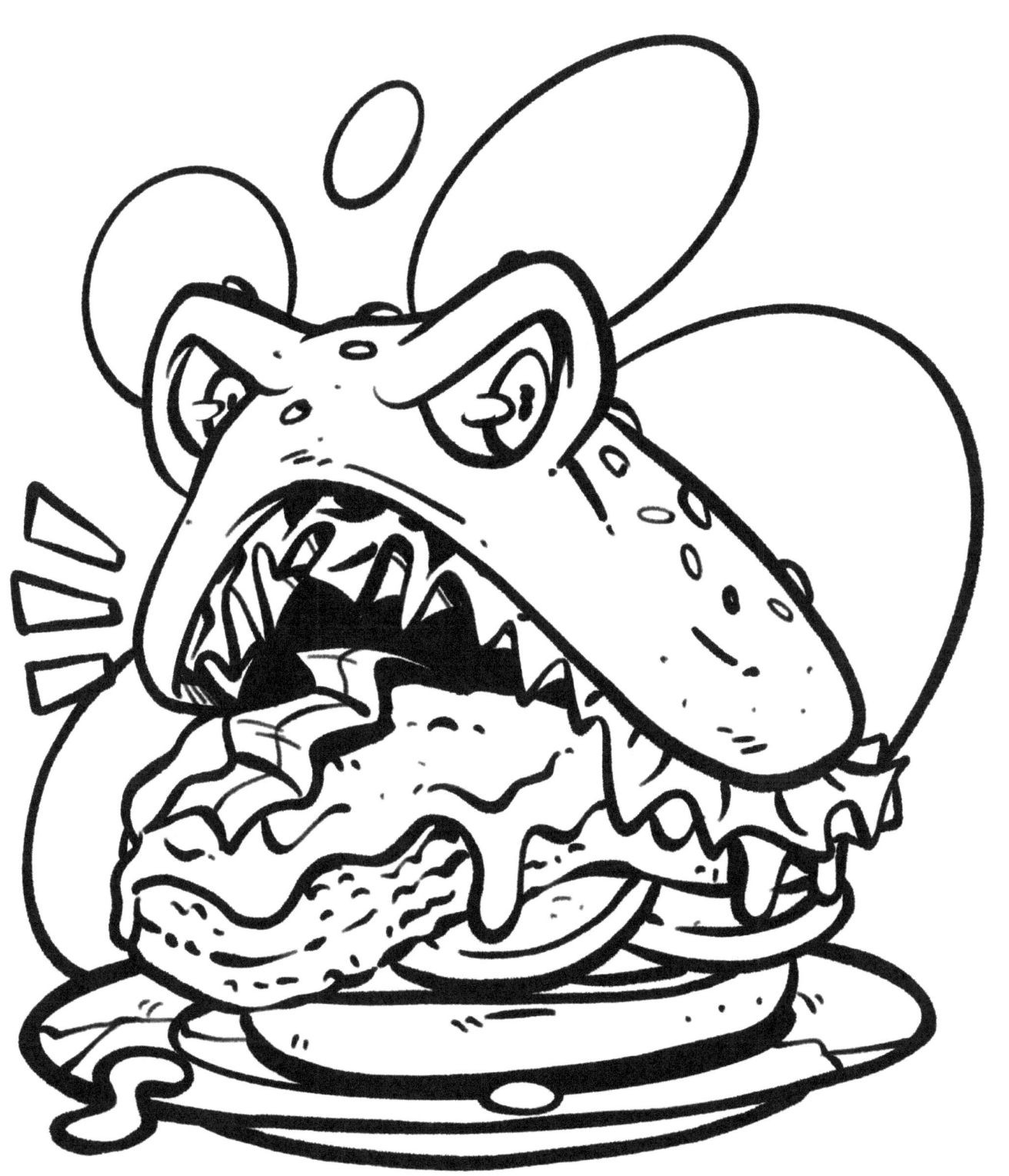

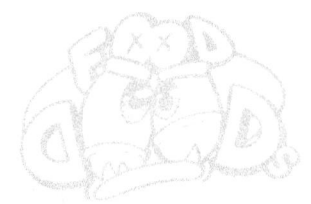

DETAIL LEVEL: LOW

DIFFICULTY: LOW

SPECIES: CROISSANT

NAME:

STRENGTH:

WEAKNESS:

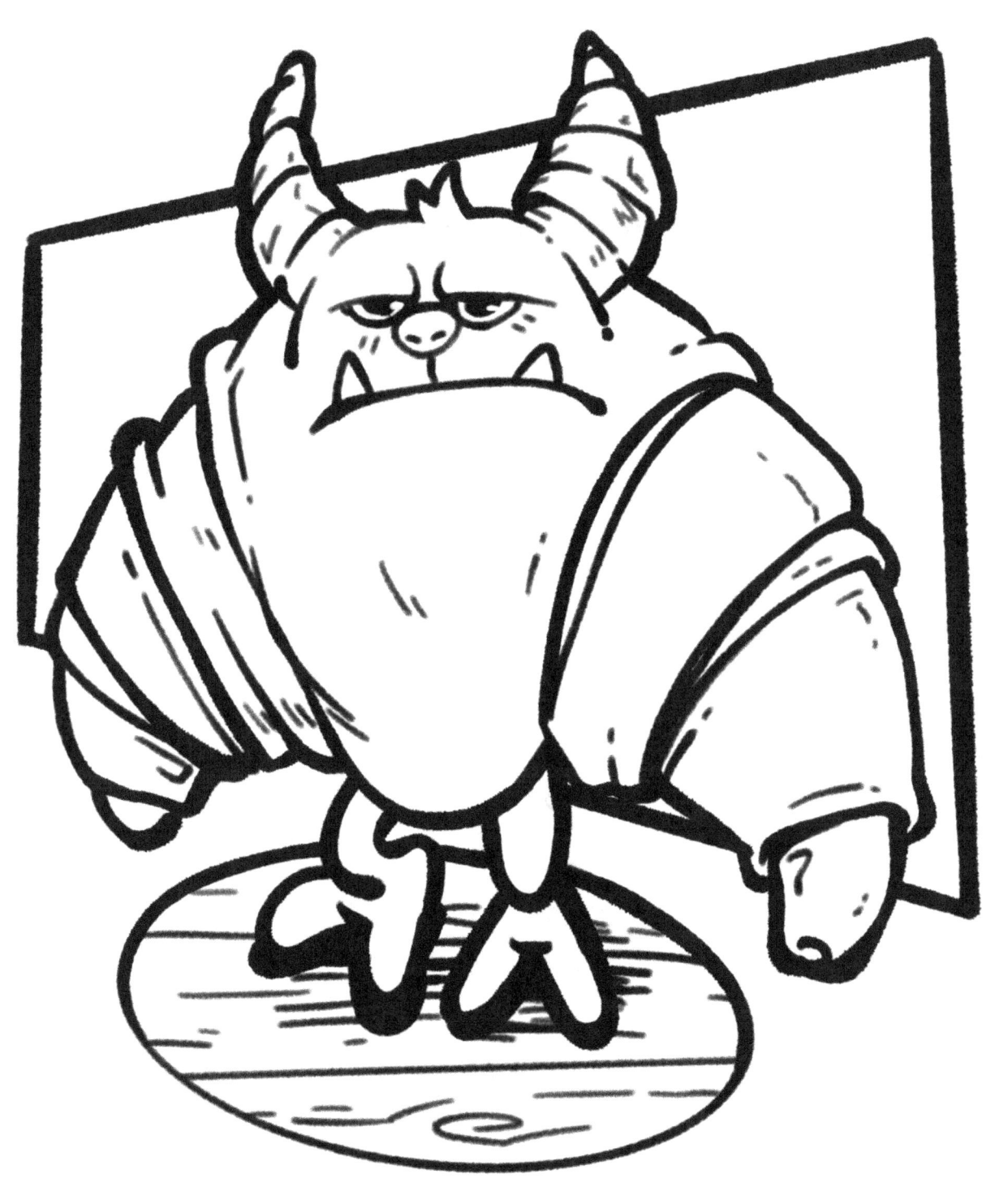

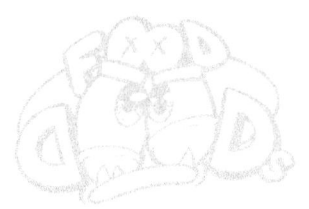

DETAIL LEVEL: LOW

DIFFICULTY: MEDIUM

SPECIES: DONUT

NAME:

STRENGTH:

WEAKNESS:

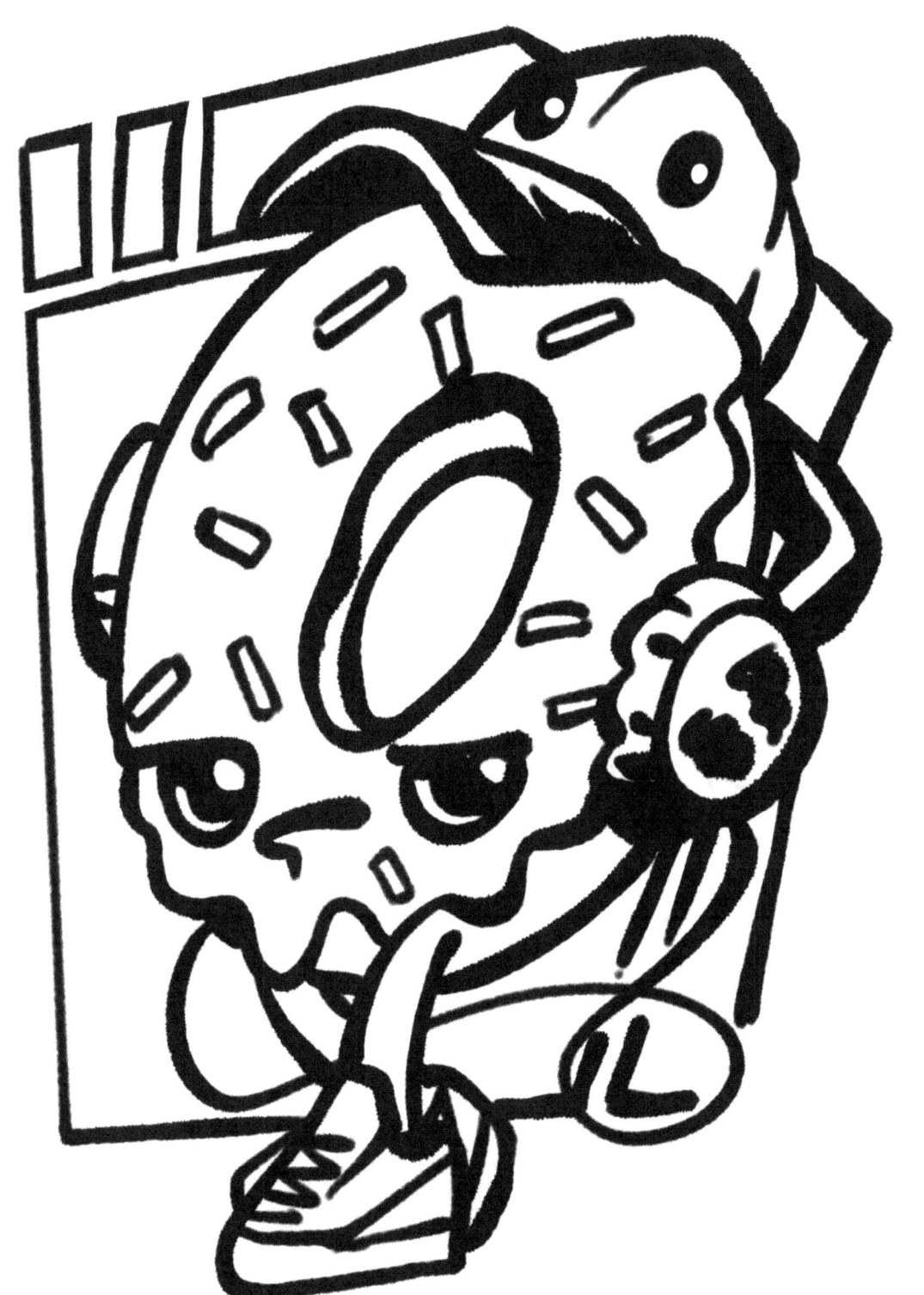

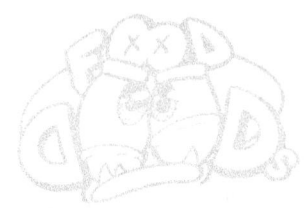

DETAIL LEVEL: HIGH

DIFFICULTY: MEDIUM

SPECIES: POTATO

NAME:

STRENGTH:

WEAKNESS:

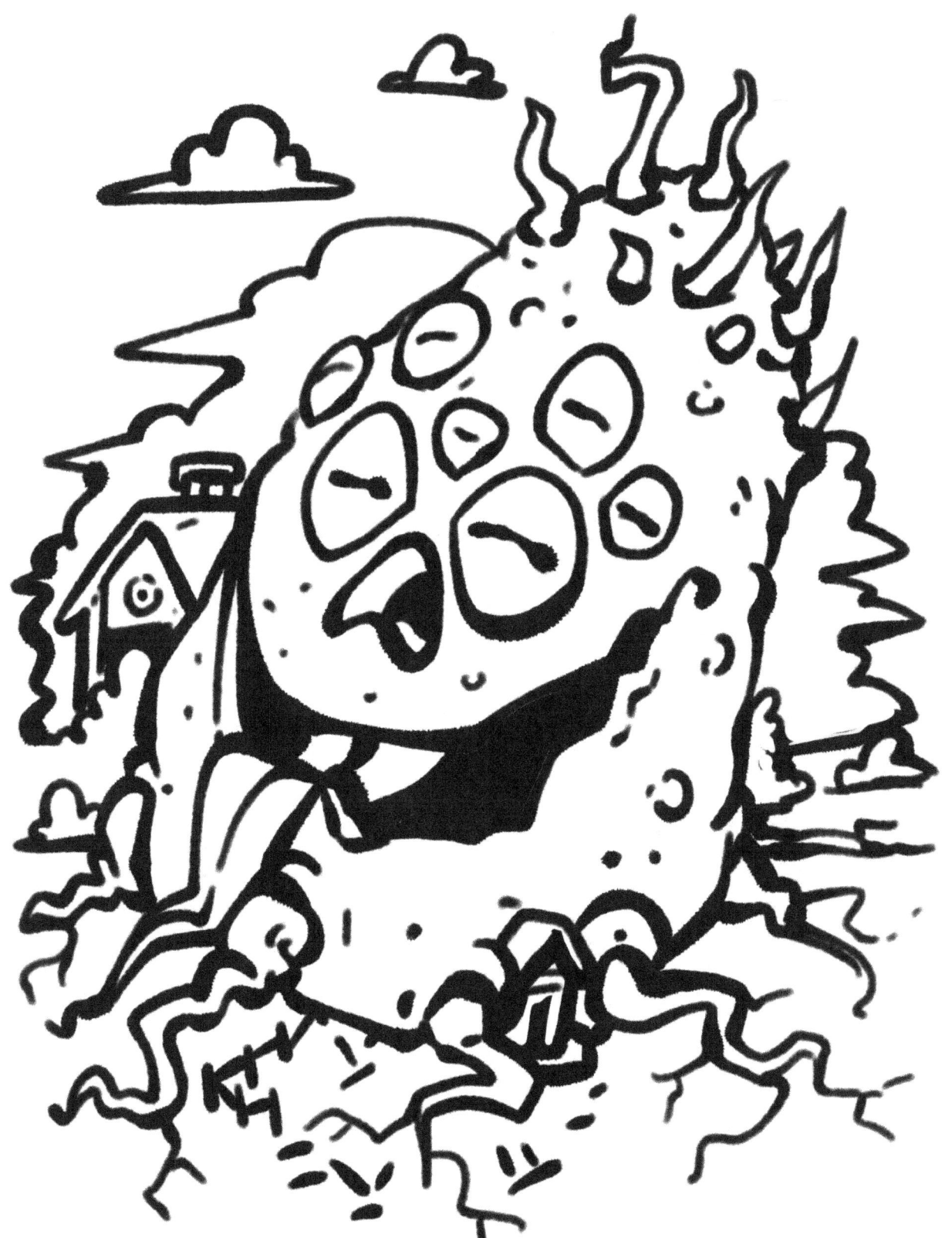

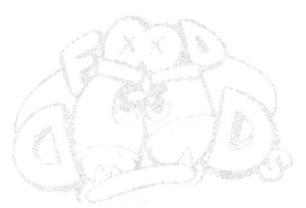

DETAIL LEVEL: LOW

DIFFICULTY: LOW

SPECIES: BEVERAGE CAN

NAME:

STRENGTH:

WEAKNESS:

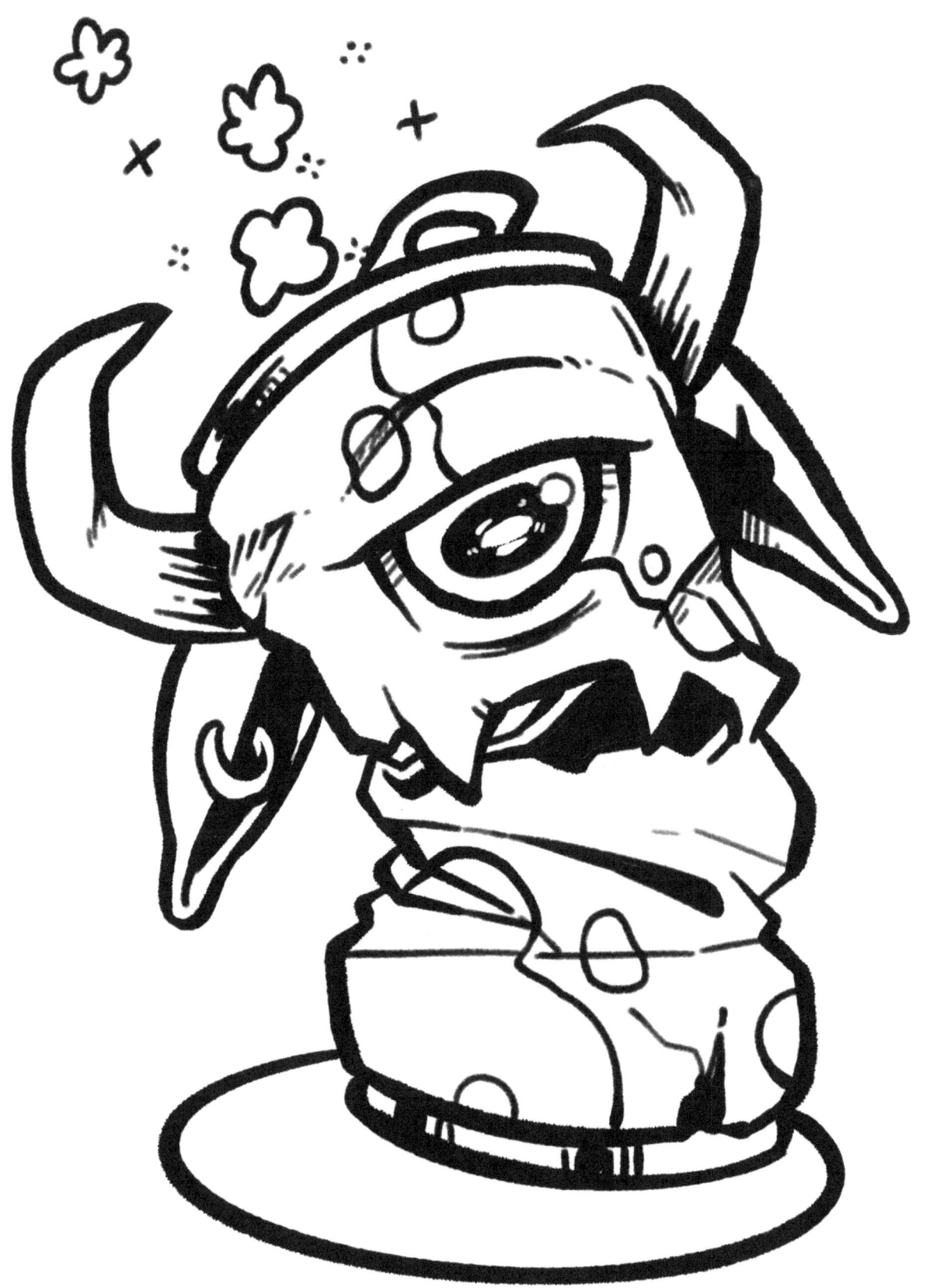

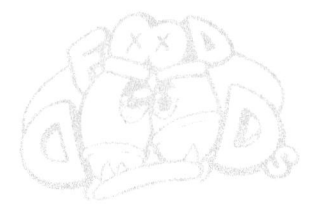

DETAIL LEVEL: LOW

DIFFICULTY: LOW

SPECIES: BURRITO

NAME:

STRENGTH:

WEAKNESS:

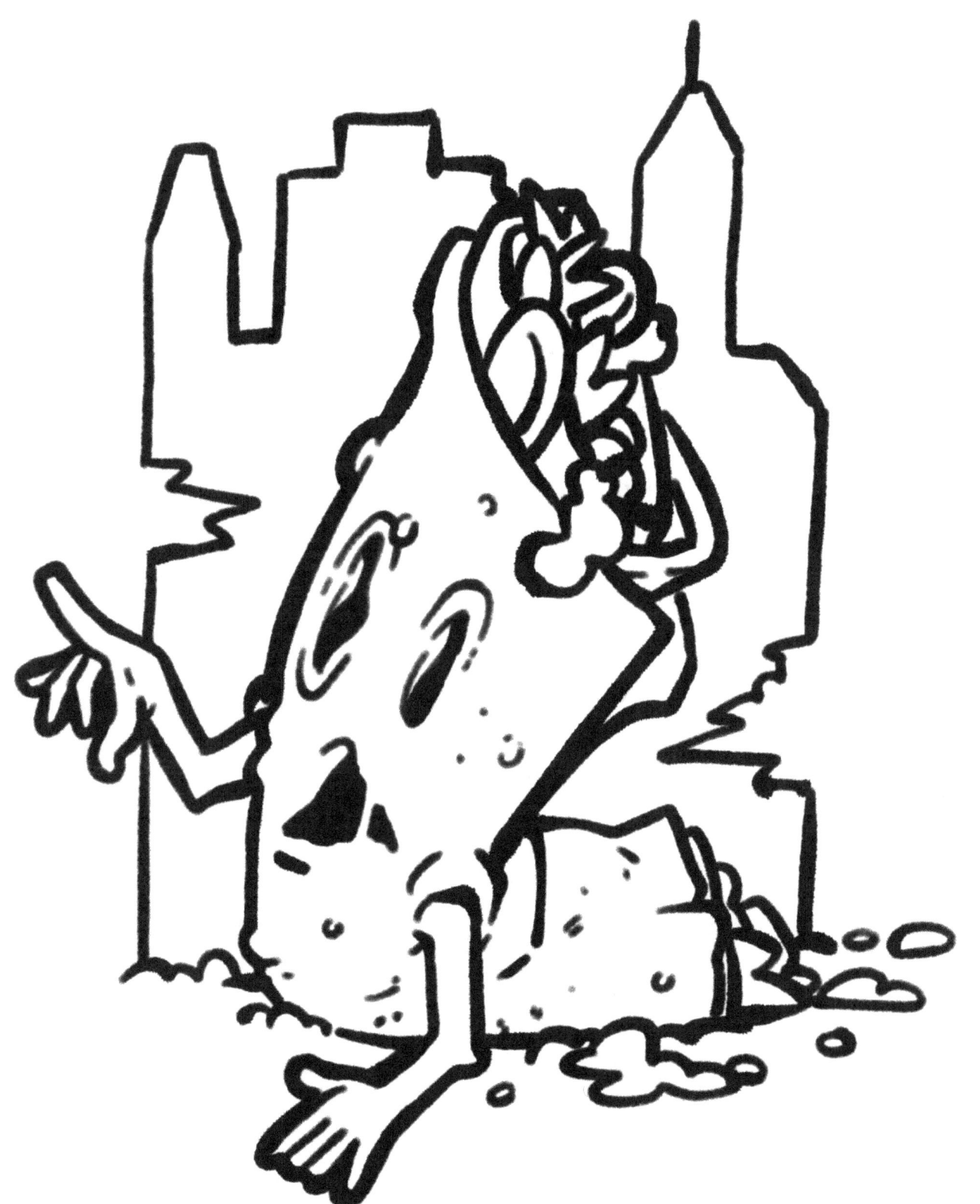

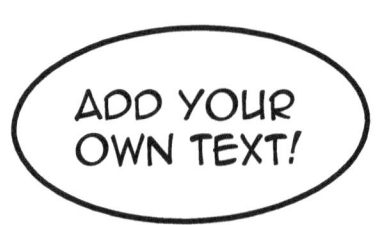
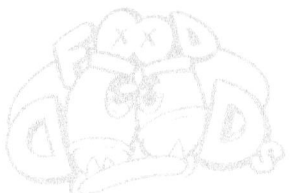

DETAIL LEVEL: HIGH

DIFFICULTY: HIGH

SPECIES: CHERRIES

NAMES:

STRENGTH:

WEAKNESS:

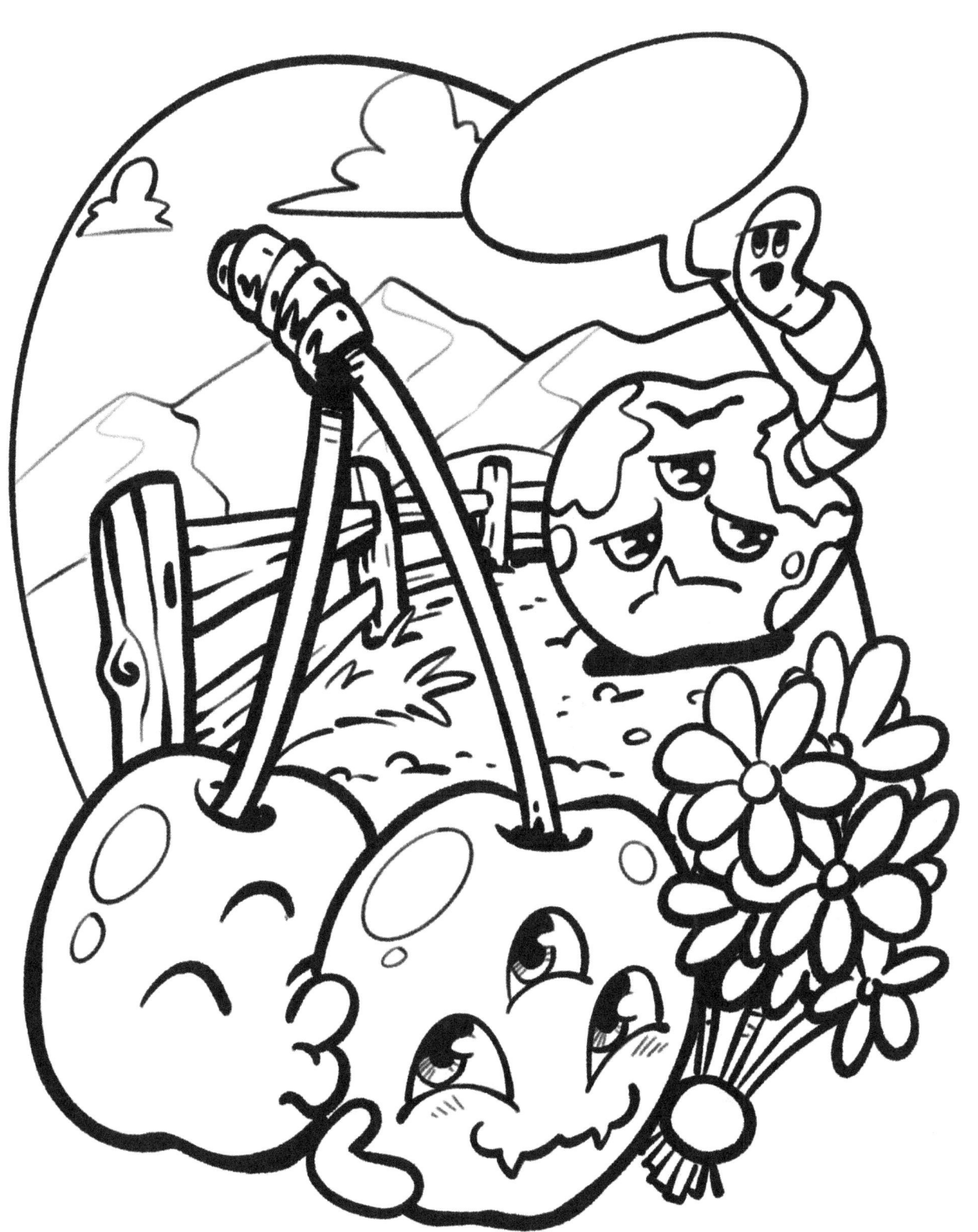

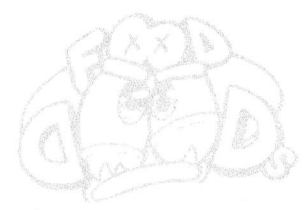

DETAIL LEVEL: LOW

DIFFICULTY: LOW

SPECIES: SODA BOTTLE

NAME:

STRENGTH:

WEAKNESS:

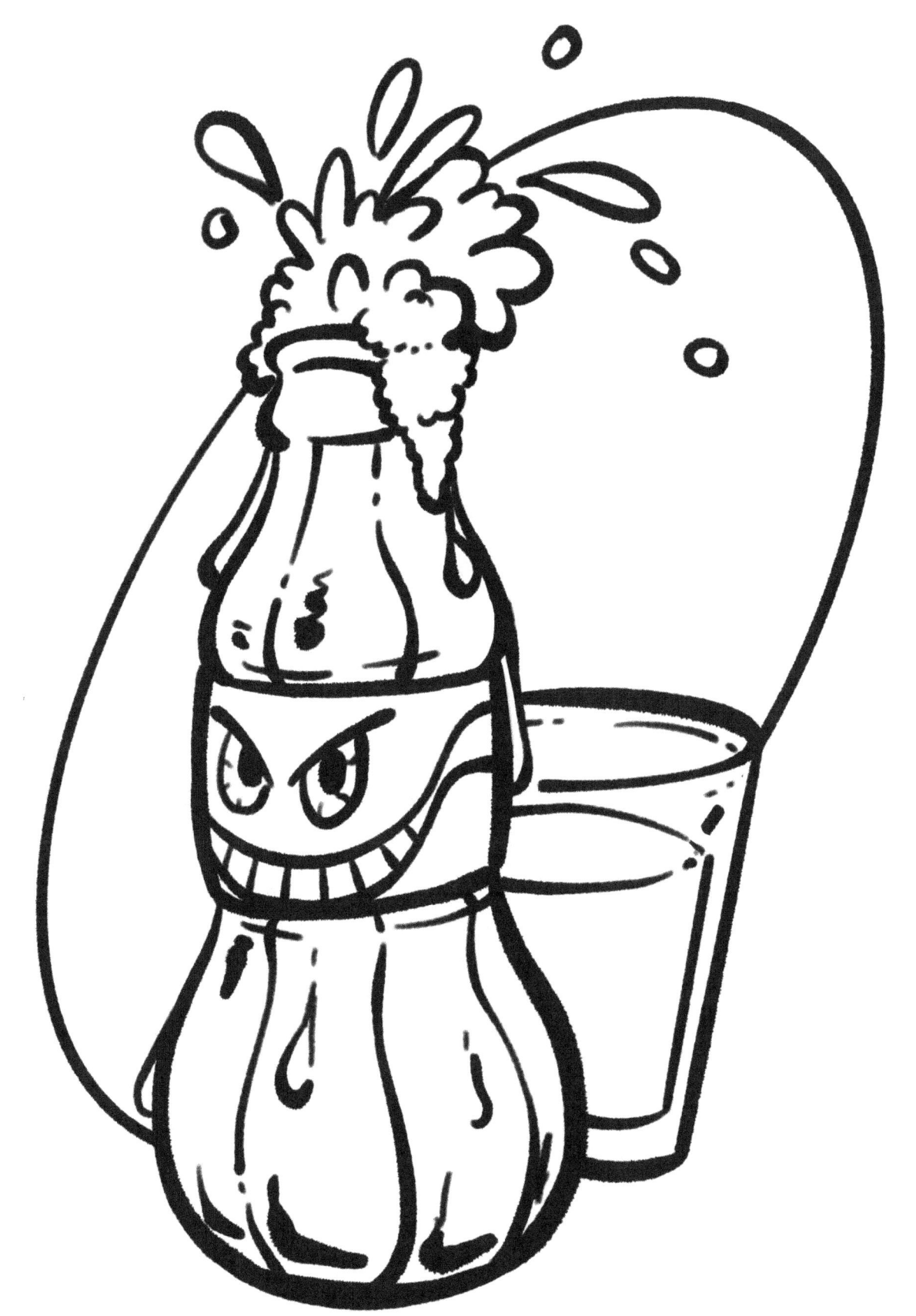

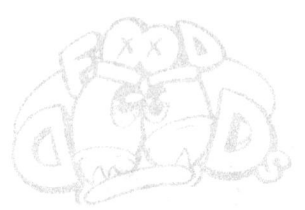

DETAIL LEVEL: LOW

DIFFICULTY: VERY LOW

SPECIES: POPSICLE

NAME:

STRENGTH:

WEAKNESS:

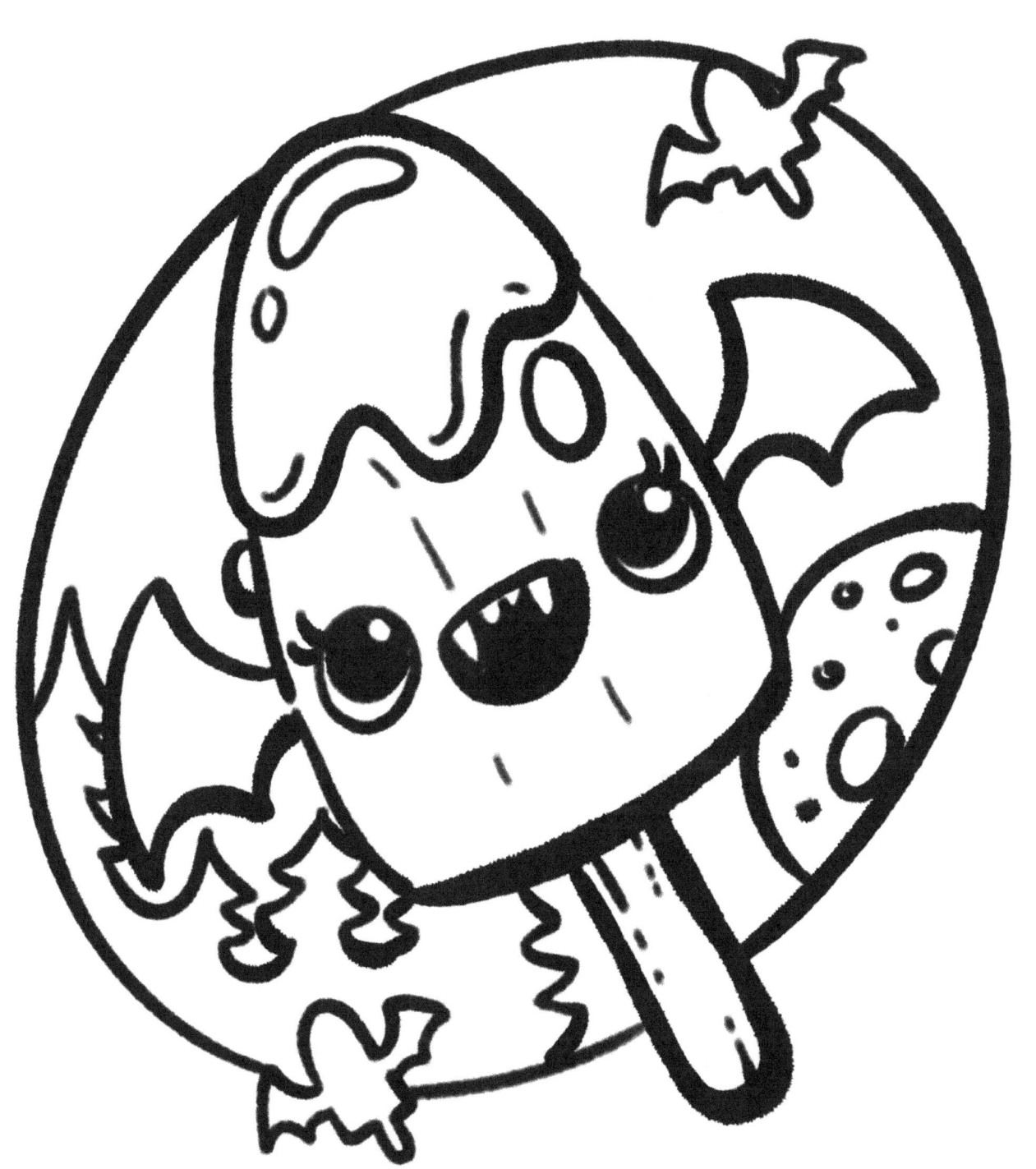

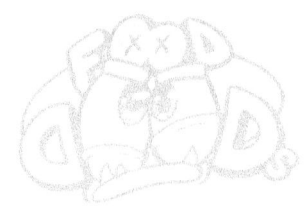

DETAIL LEVEL: MEDIUM

DIFFICULTY: LOW

SPECIES: CUPCAKE

NAME:

STRENGTH:

WEAKNESS:

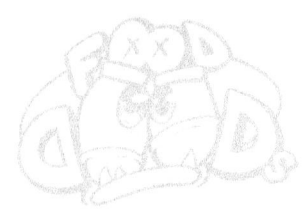

DETAIL LEVEL: VERY HIGH

DIFFICULTY: VERY HIGH

SPECIES: PIZZA

NAME:

STRENGTH:

WEAKNESS:

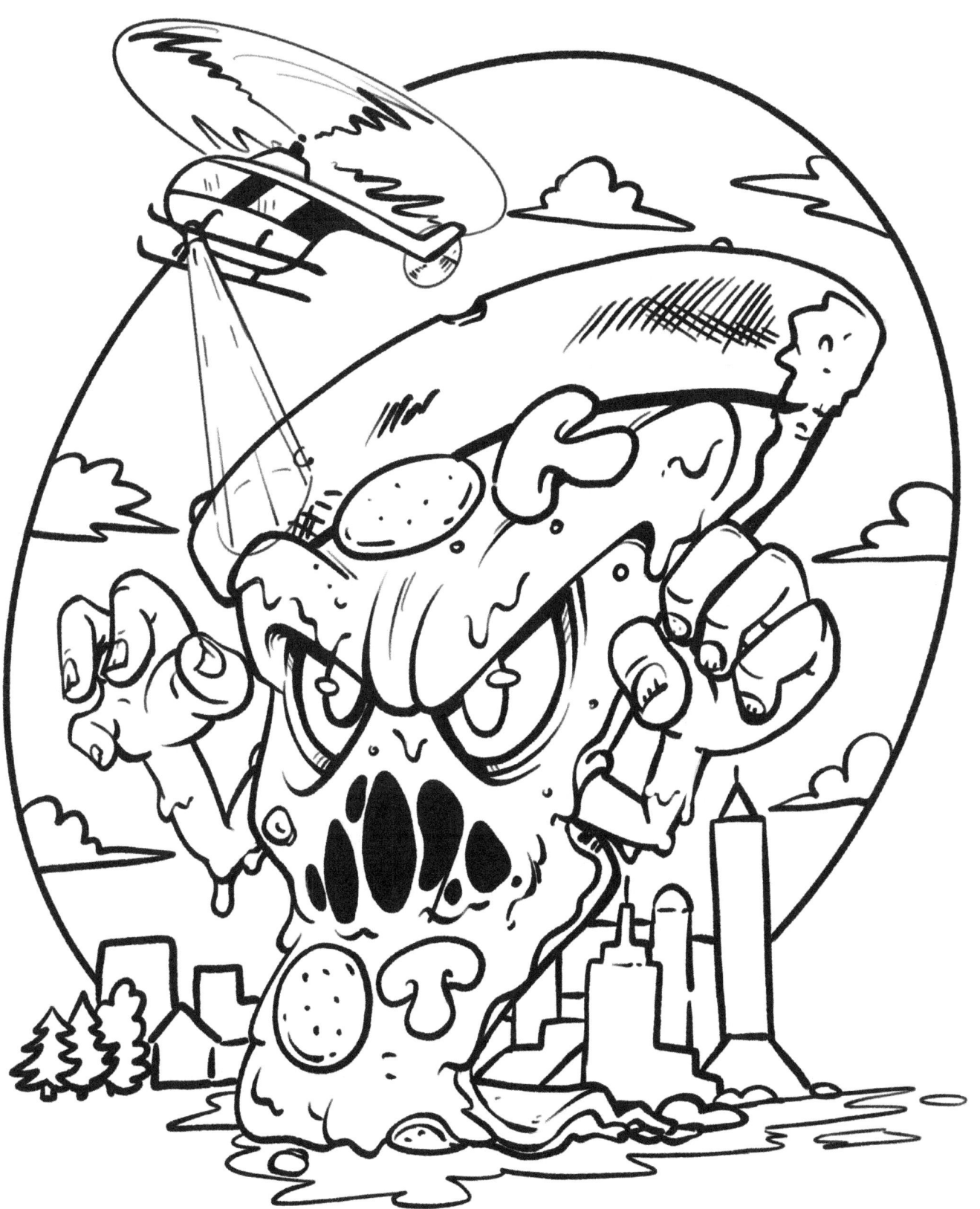

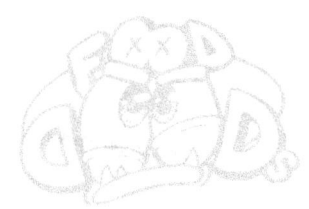

DETAIL LEVEL: MEDIUM

DIFFICULTY: LOW

SPECIES: TORTILLA CHIPS

NAME:

STRENGTH:

WEAKNESS:

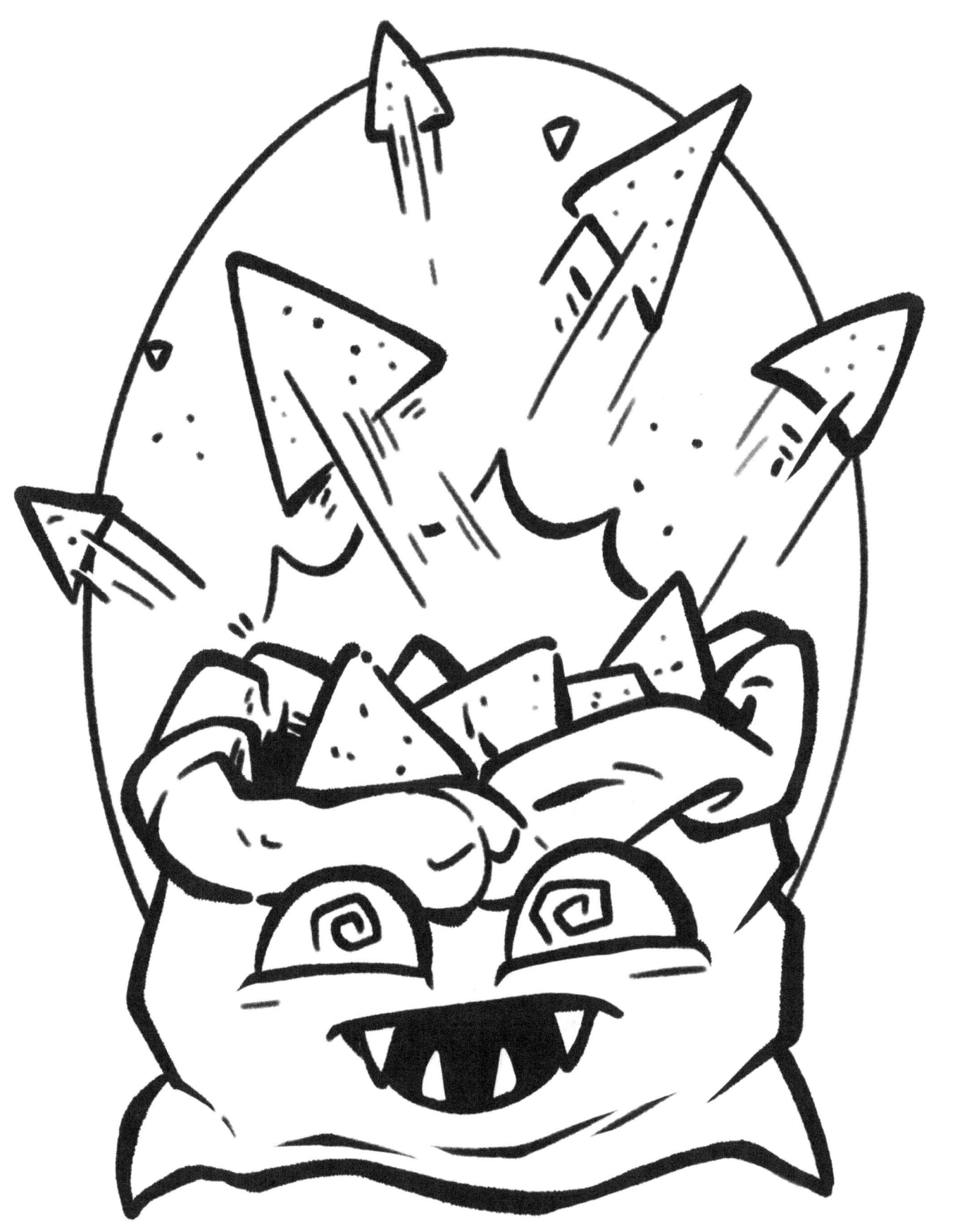

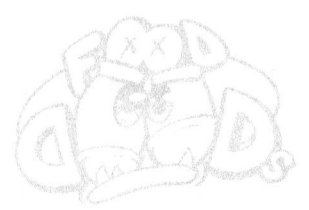

DETAIL LEVEL: LOW

DIFFICULTY: MEDIUM

SPECIES: BANANA

NAME:

STRENGTH:

WEAKNESS:

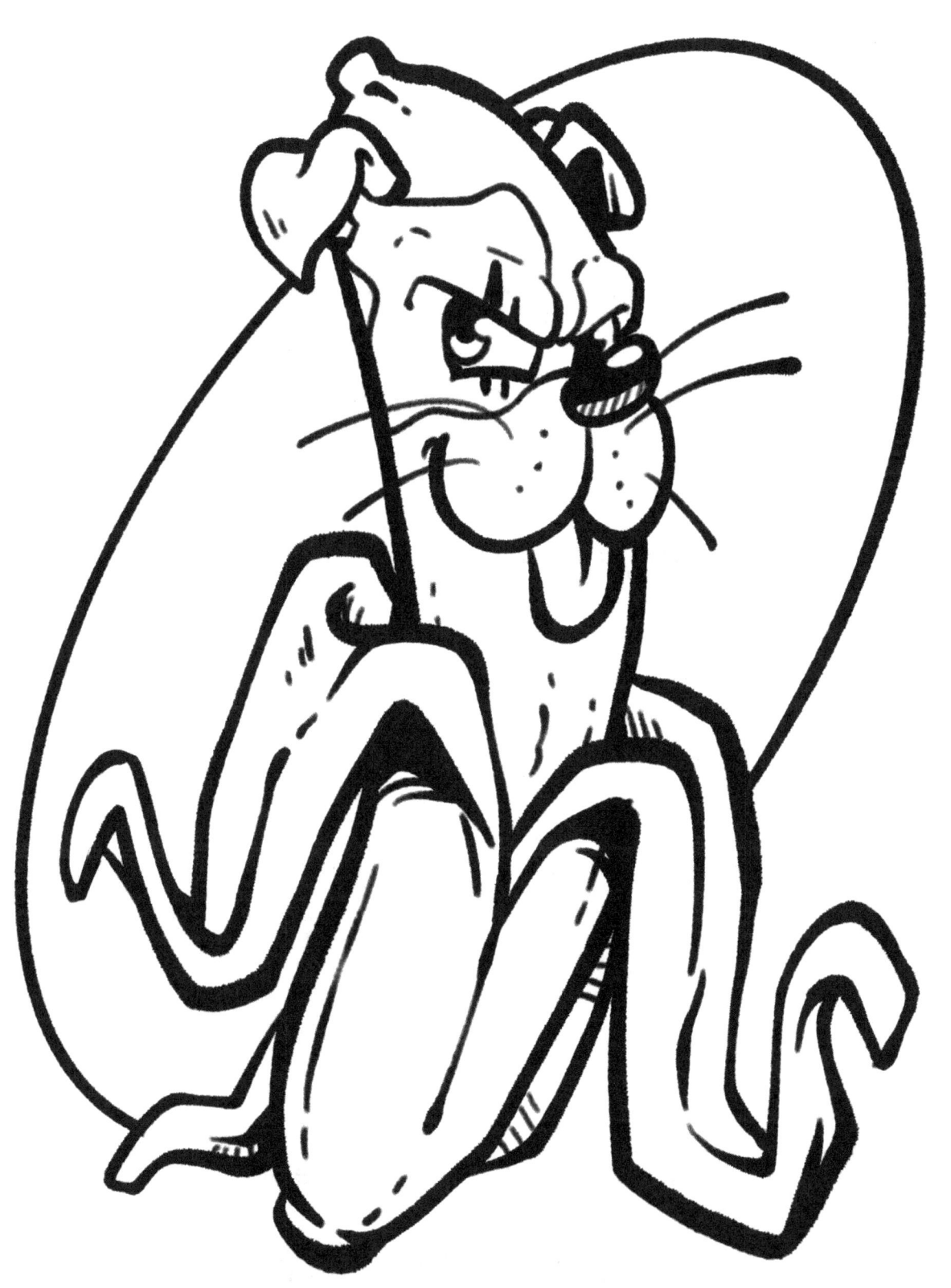

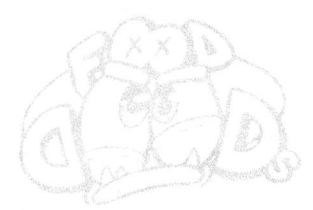

DETAIL LEVEL: LOW

DIFFICULTY: MEDIUM

SPECIES: EGG

NAME:

STRENGTH:

WEAKNESS:

E-MAIL ME YOUR CRAZY MONSTERS AND IDEAS FOR NEW MONSTERS AT:

TOMISLAVARTZ+BOOK@GMAIL.COM

© Tomislav Artz | tomislav.at | Instagram: jtomislav

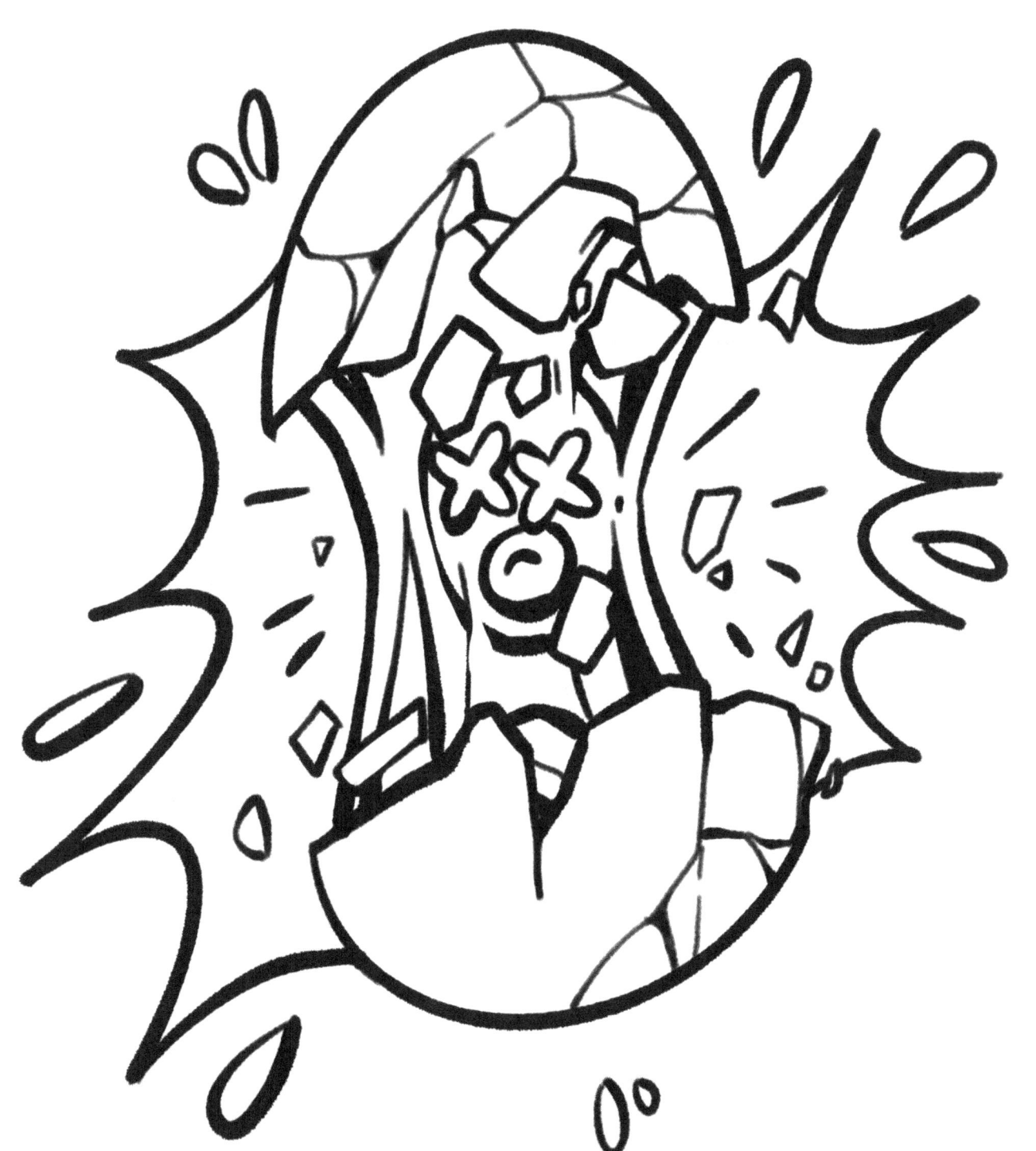

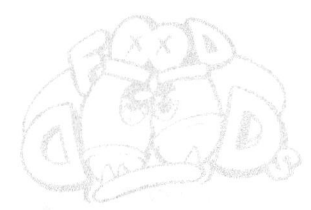

DETAIL LEVEL: HIGH

DIFFICULTY: MEDIUM

SPECIES: POPCORN

NAME:

STRENGTH:

WEAKNESS:

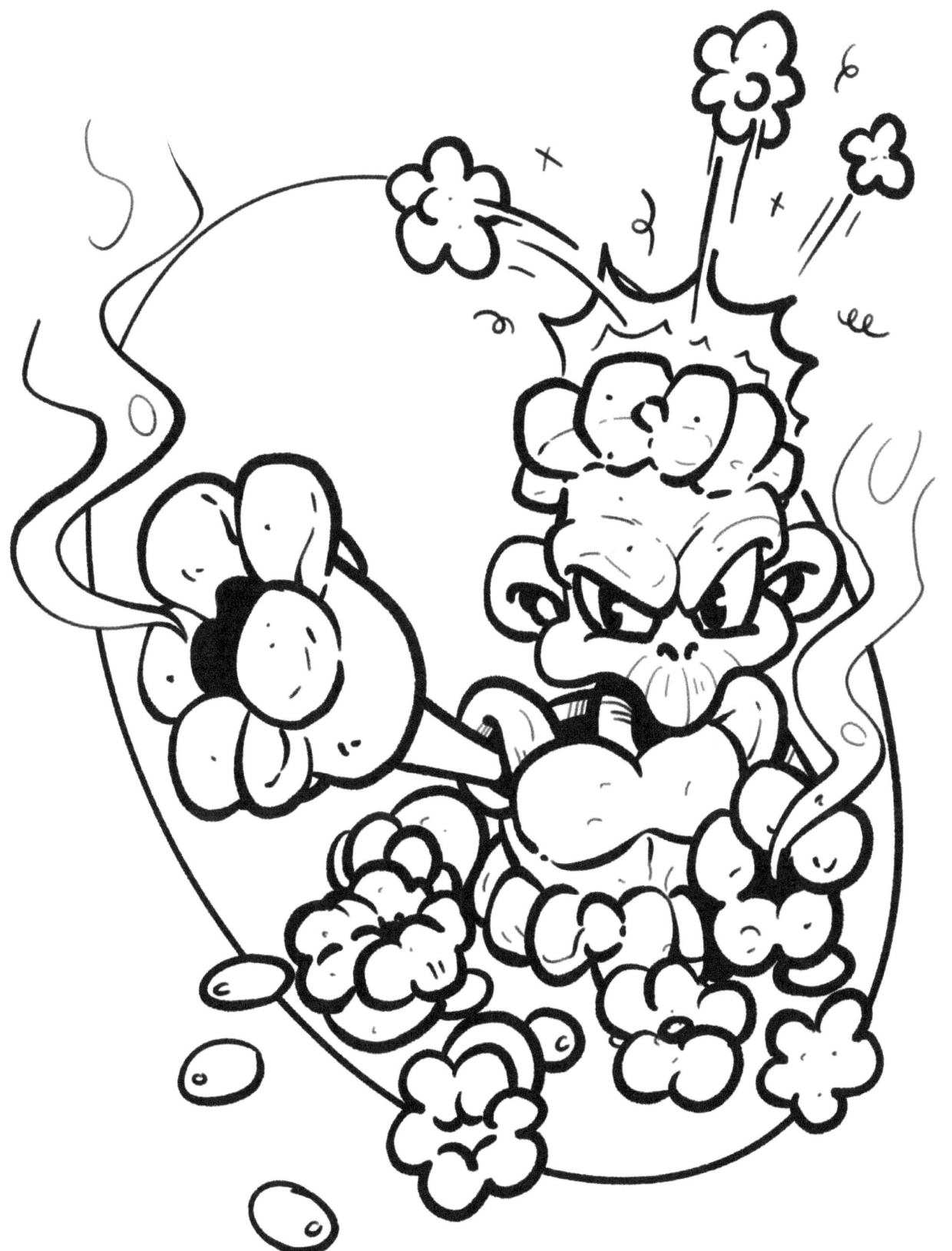

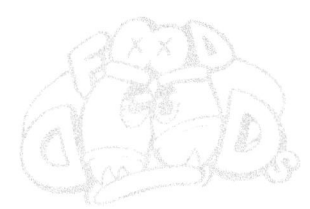

DETAIL LEVEL: HIGH

DIFFICULTY: MEDIUM

SPECIES: PINEAPPLE

NAME:

STRENGTH:

WEAKNESS:

© Tomislav Artz | tomislav.at | Instagram: jtomislav

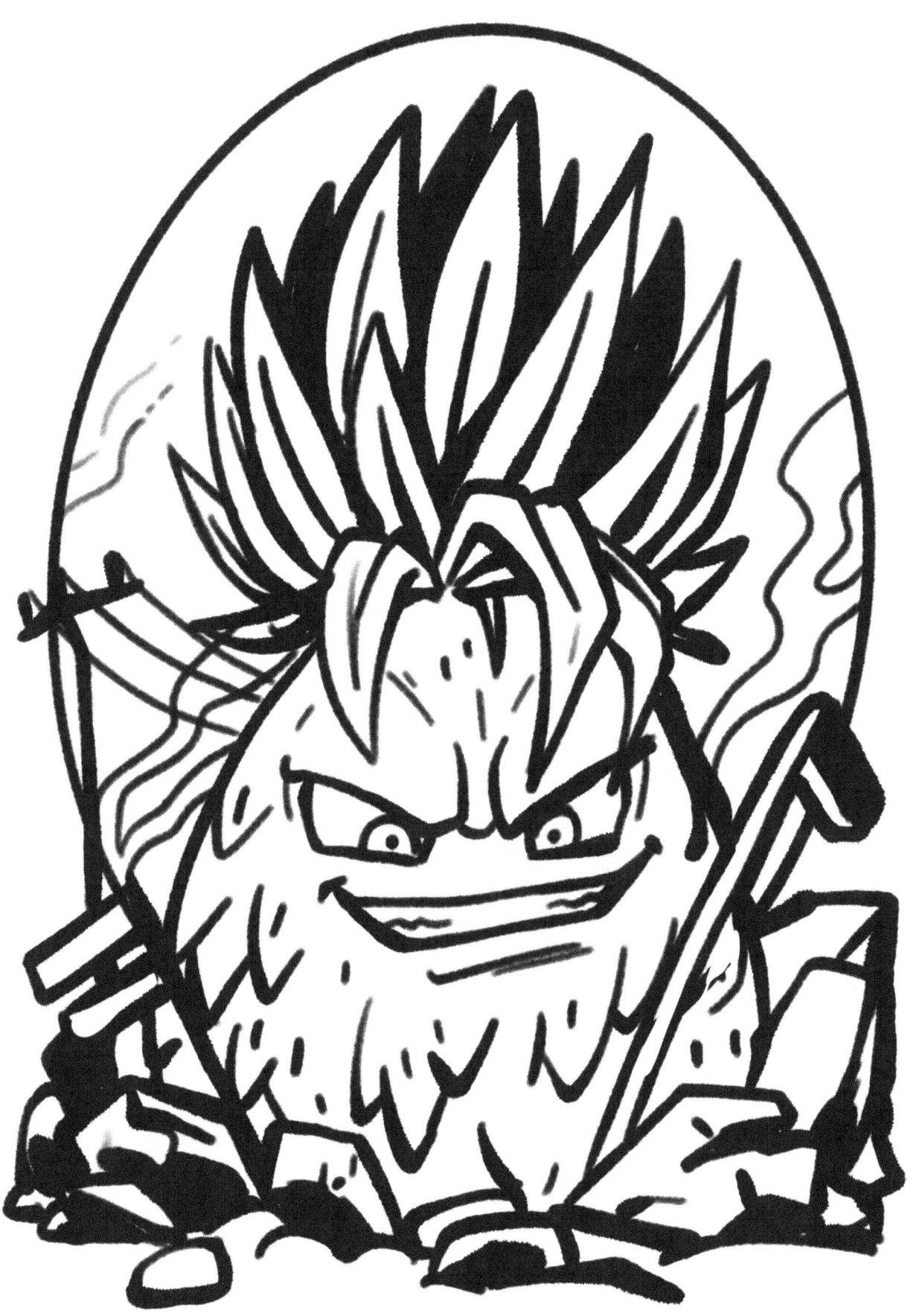

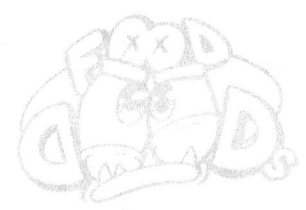

DETAIL LEVEL: LOW

DIFFICULTY: LOW

SPECIES: GRAPES

NAME:

STRENGTH:

WEAKNESS:

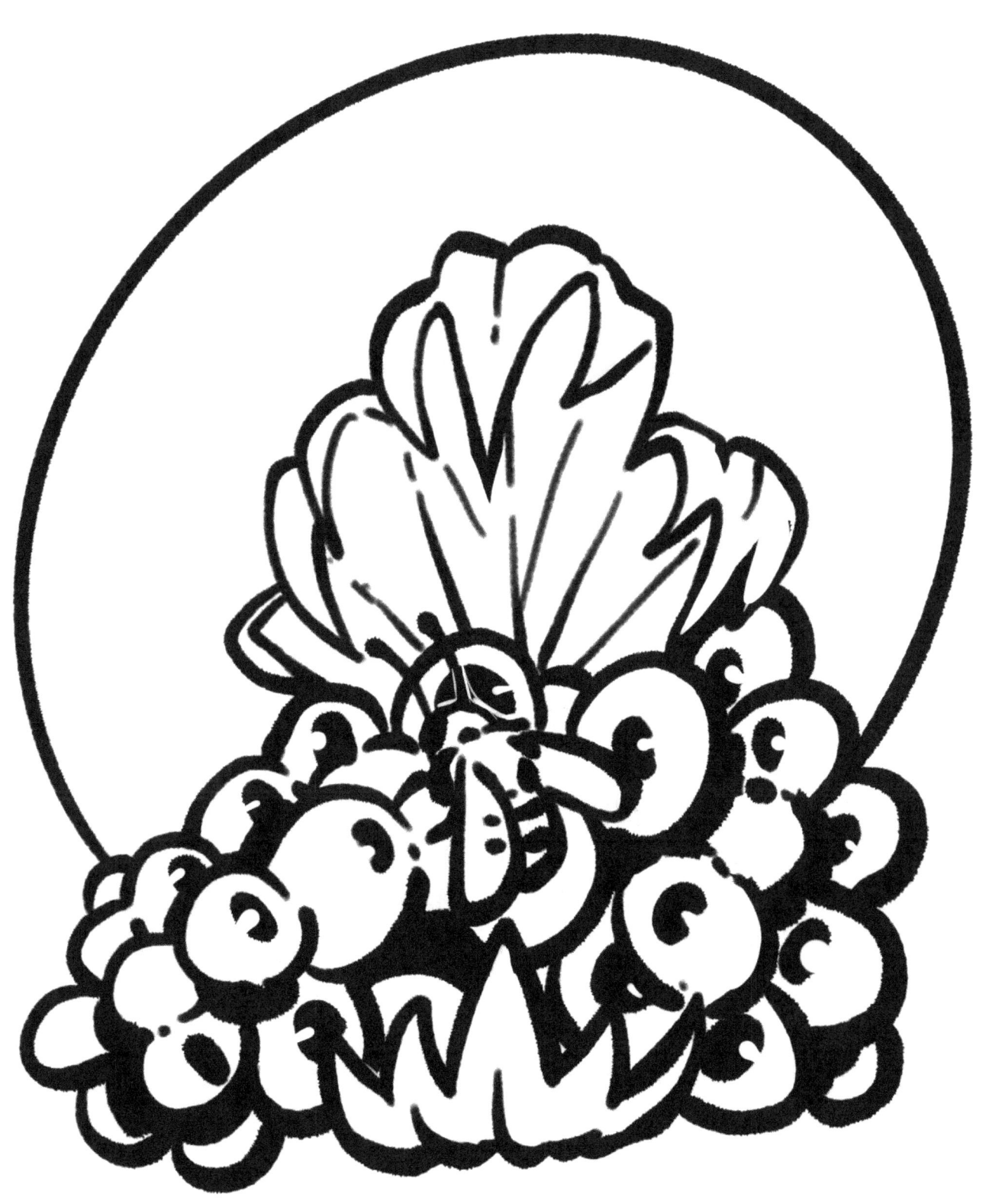

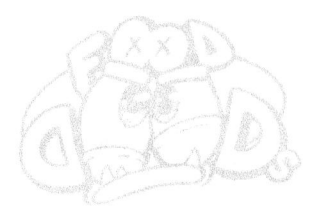

DETAIL LEVEL: HIGH

DIFFICULTY: MEDIUM

SPECIES: APPLE

NAME:

STRENGTH:

WEAKNESS:

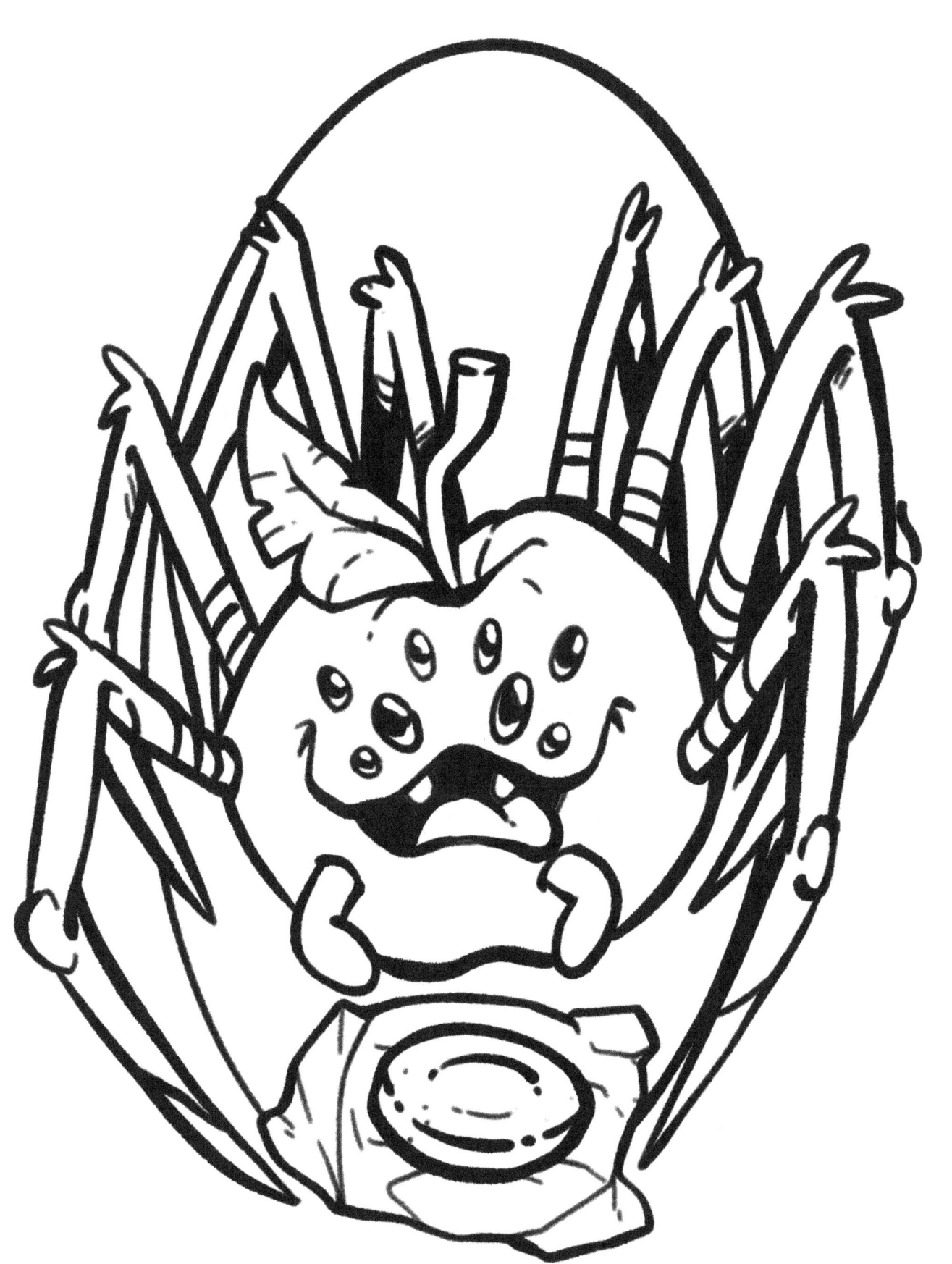

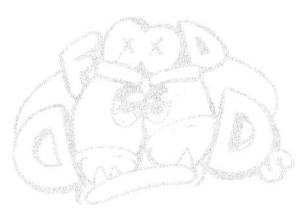

DETAIL LEVEL: HIGH

DIFFICULTY: HIGH

SPECIES: BREAD

NAME:

STRENGTH:

WEAKNESS:

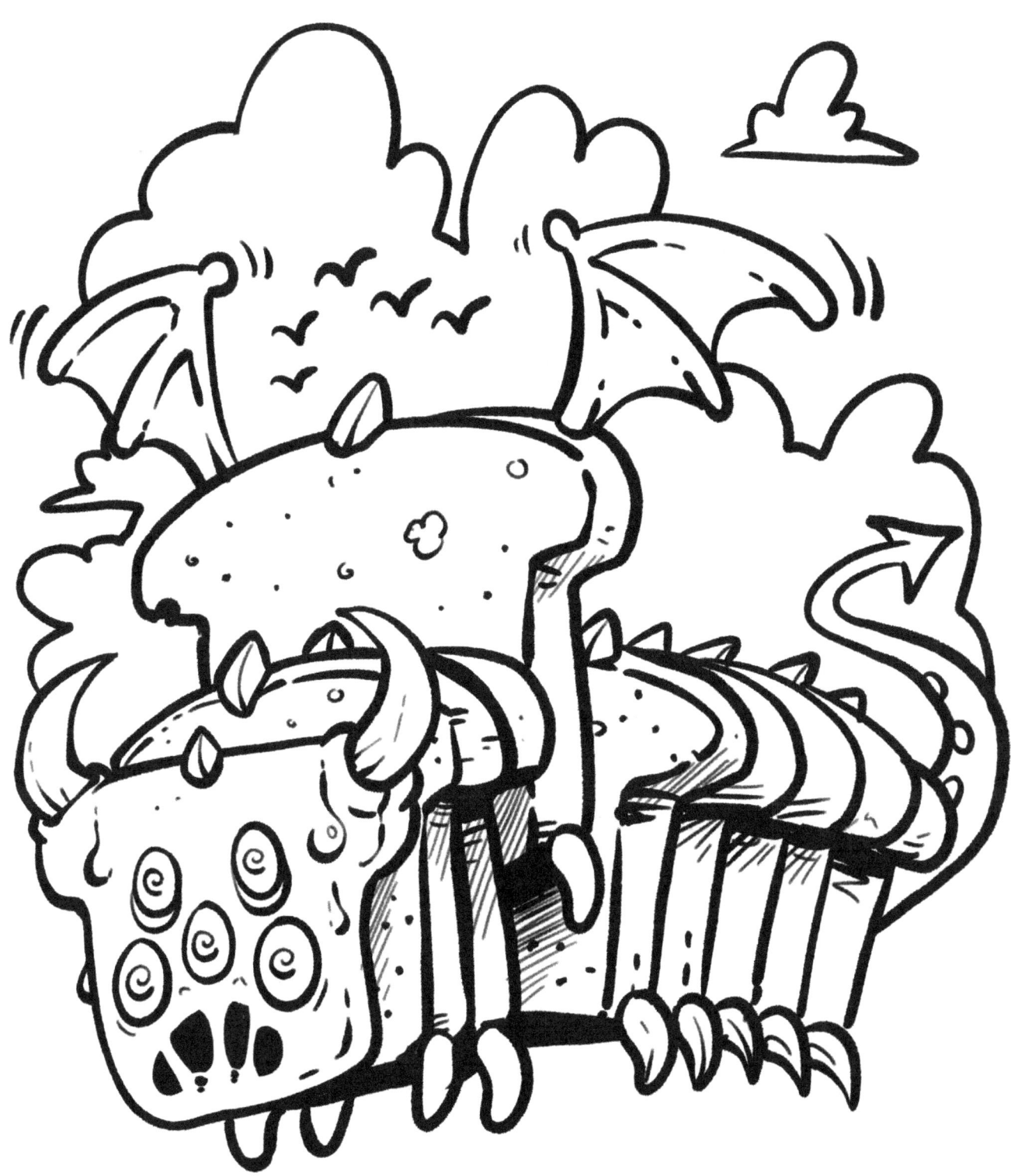

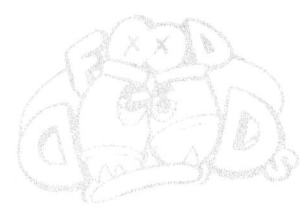

DETAIL LEVEL: MEDIUM

DIFFICULTY: MEDIUM

SPECIES: HOT DOG

NAME:

STRENGTH:

WEAKNESS:

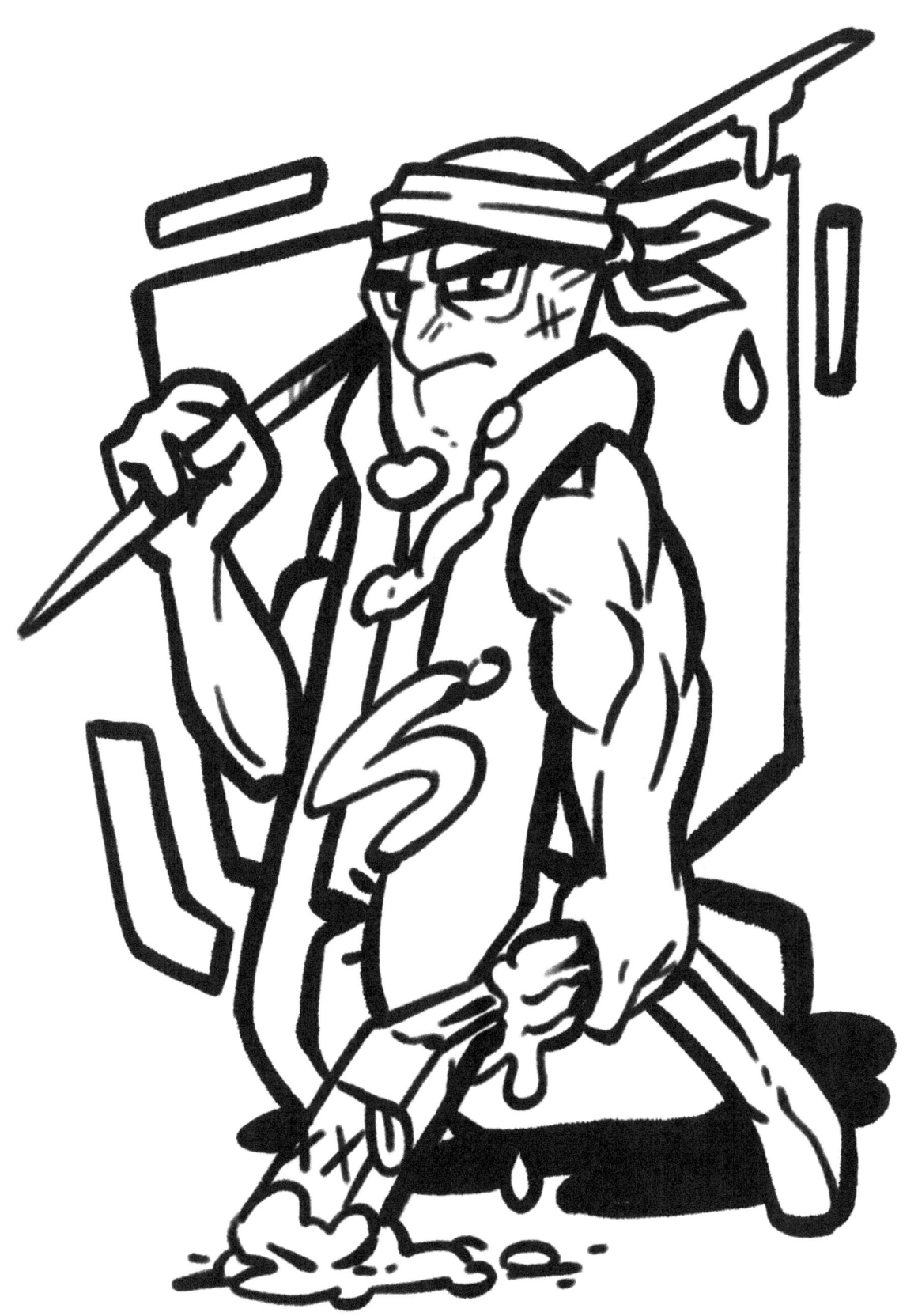

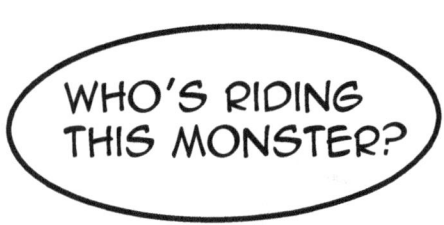
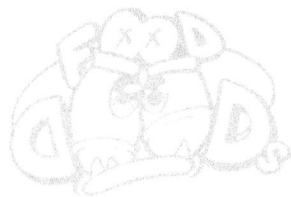

DETAIL LEVEL: HIGH

DIFFICULTY: HIGH

SPECIES: PEAR

NAME:

RIDER:

STRENGTH:

WEAKNESS:

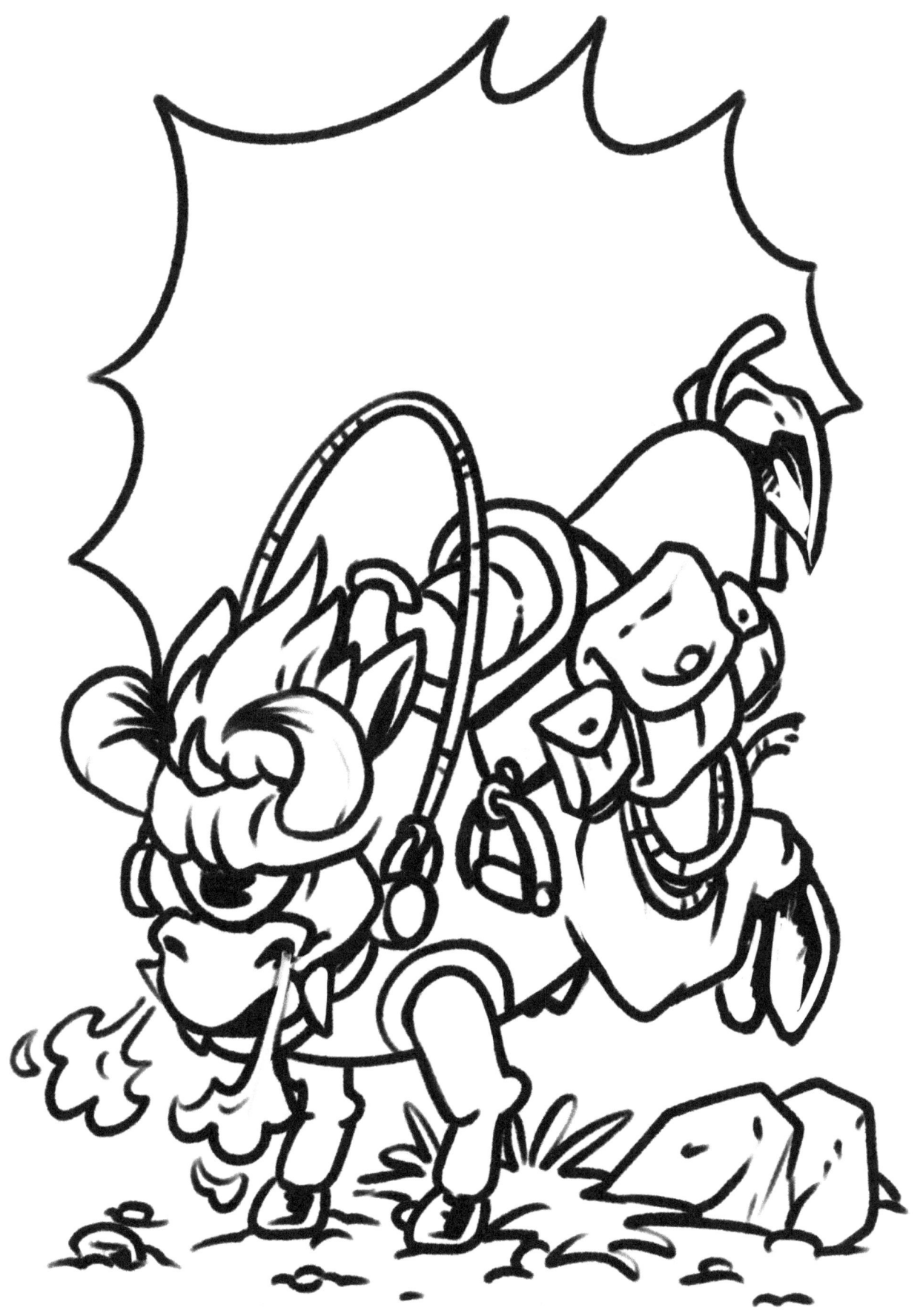

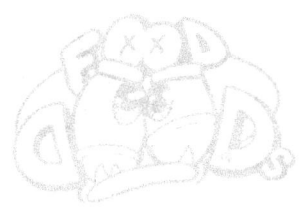

DETAIL LEVEL: HIGH

DIFFICULTY: HIGH

SPECIES: PUMPKIN

NAME:

STRENGTH:

WEAKNESS:

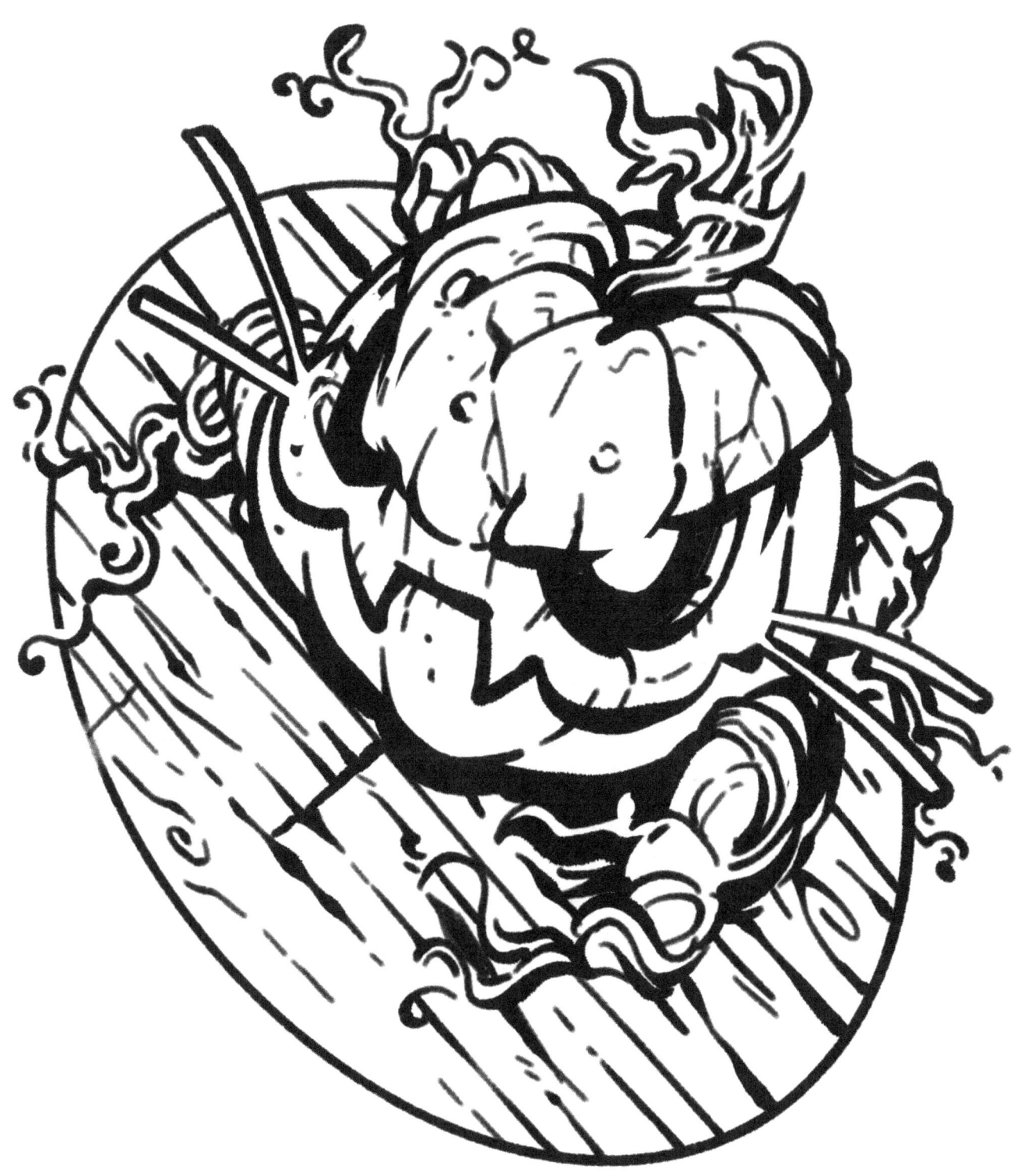

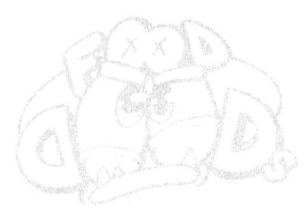

DETAIL LEVEL: LOW

DIFFICULTY: VERY LOW

SPECIES: SAUSAGE

NAME:

STRENGTH:

WEAKNESS:

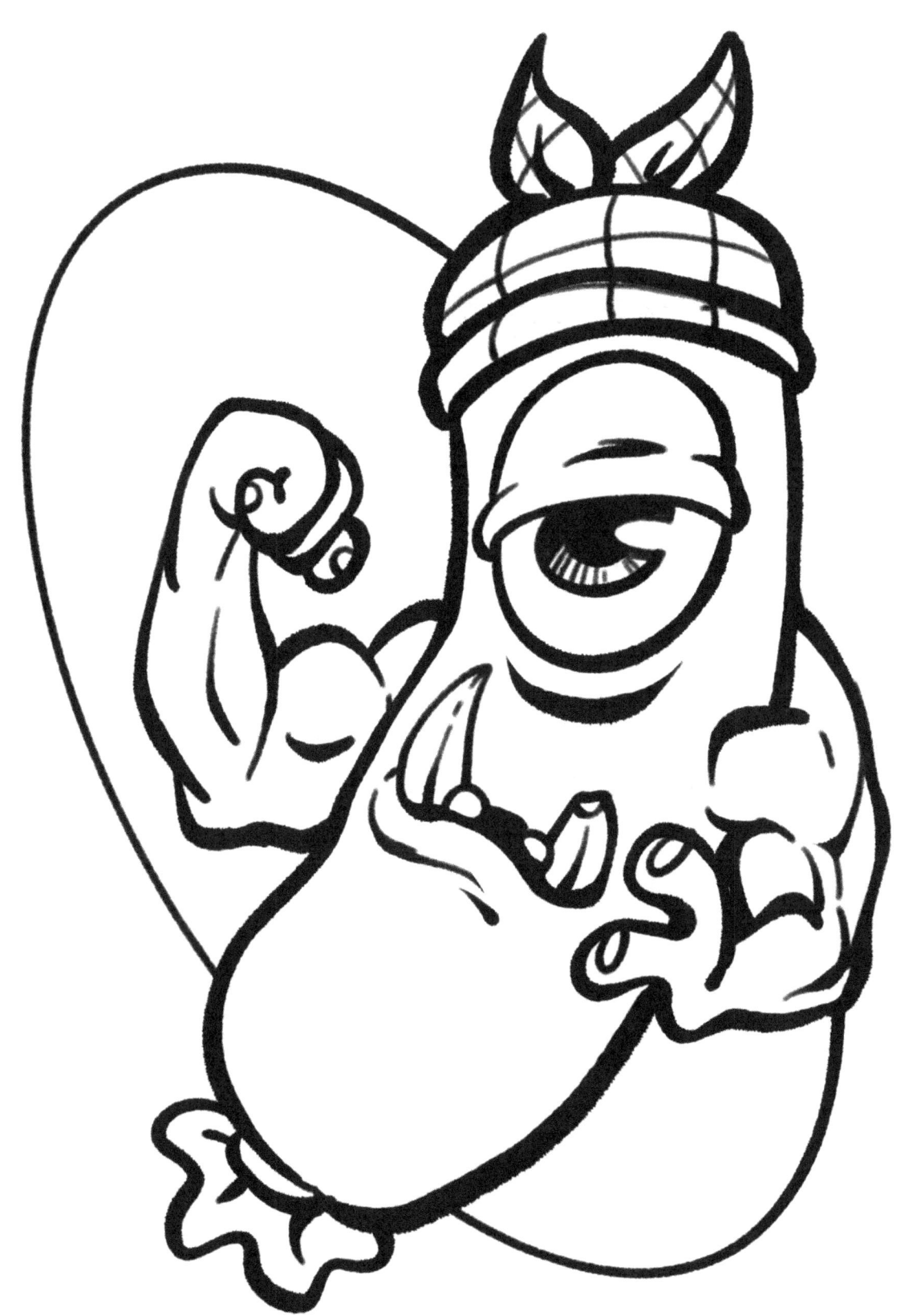

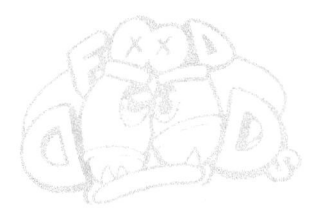

DETAIL LEVEL: MEDIUM

DIFFICULTY: MEDIUM

SPECIES: SLUSHY

NAME:

STRENGTH:

WEAKNESS:

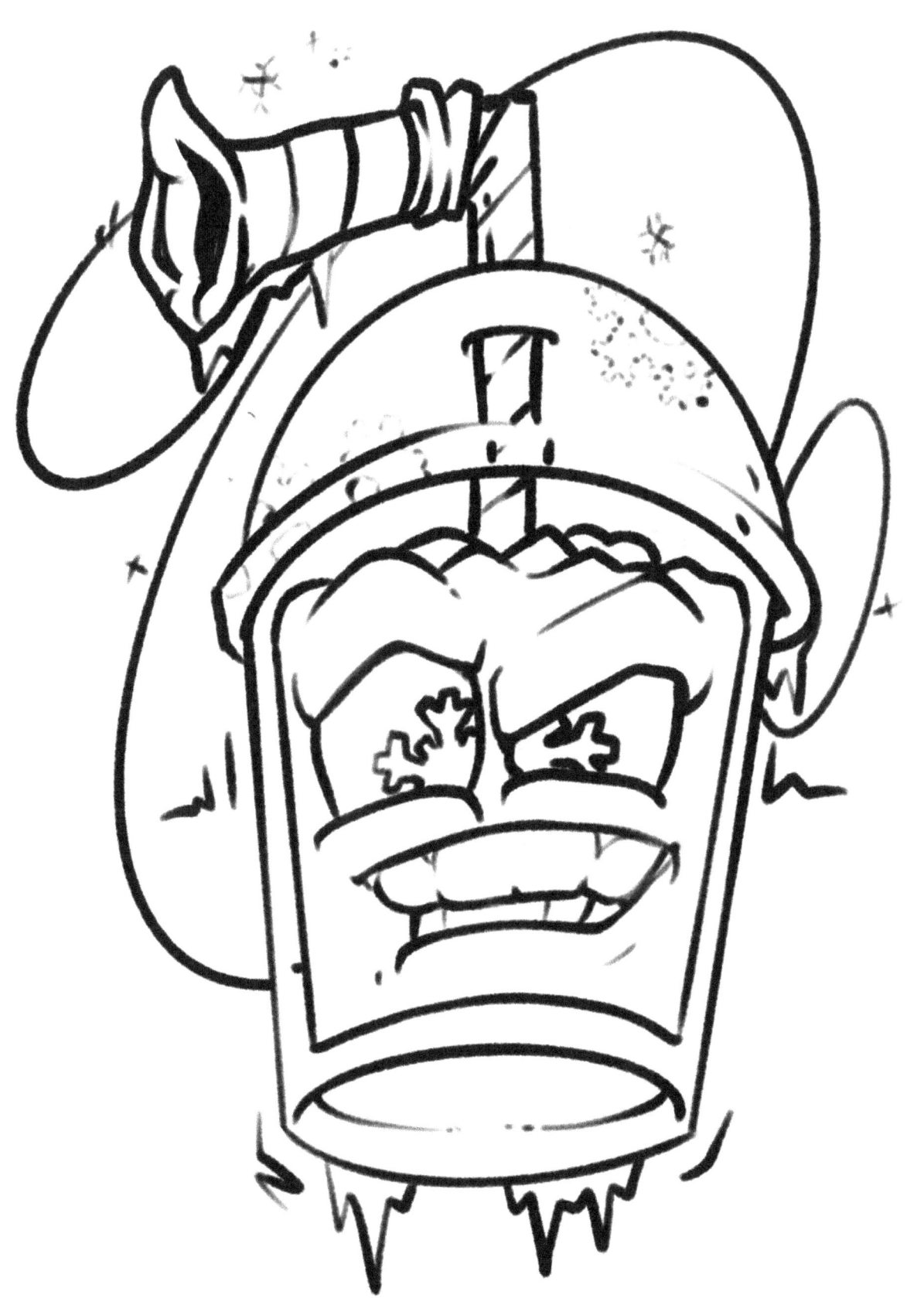

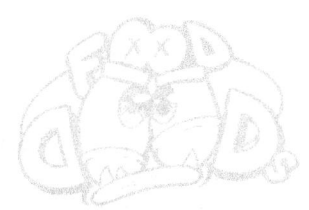

DETAIL LEVEL: VERY HIGH

DIFFICULTY: MEDIUM

SPECIES: SPAGHETTI

NAME:

STRENGTH:

WEAKNESS:

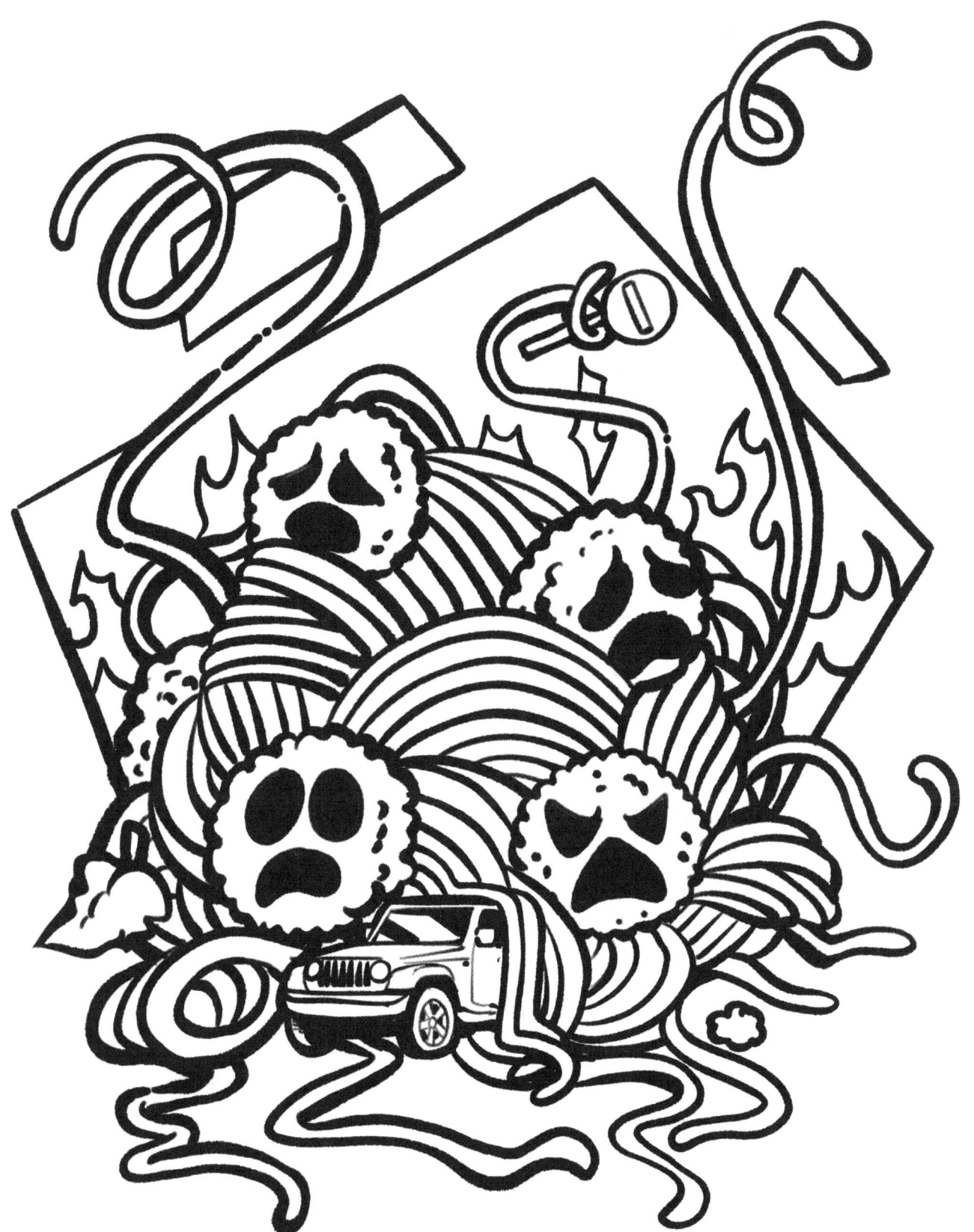

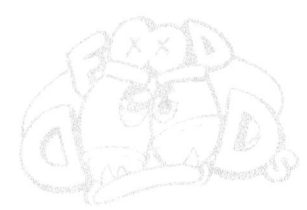

DETAIL LEVEL: HIGH

DIFFICULTY: MEDIUM

SPECIES: SUSHI

NAME:

STRENGTH:

WEAKNESS:

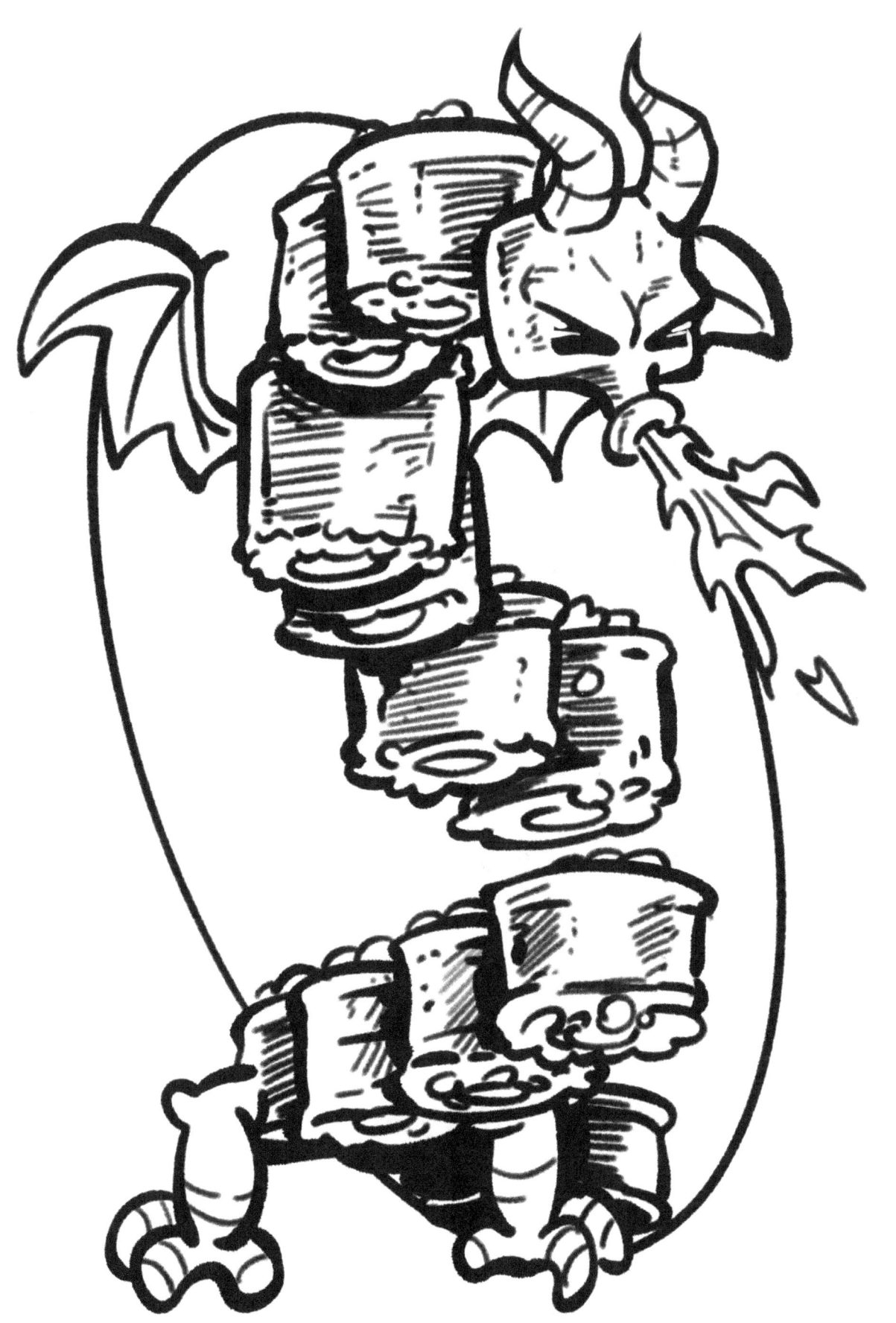

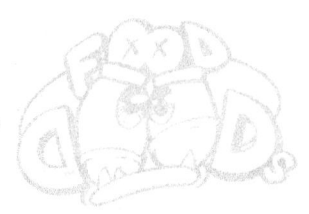

DETAIL LEVEL: MEDIUM

DIFFICULTY: LOW

SPECIES: TACO

NAME:

STRENGTH:

WEAKNESS:

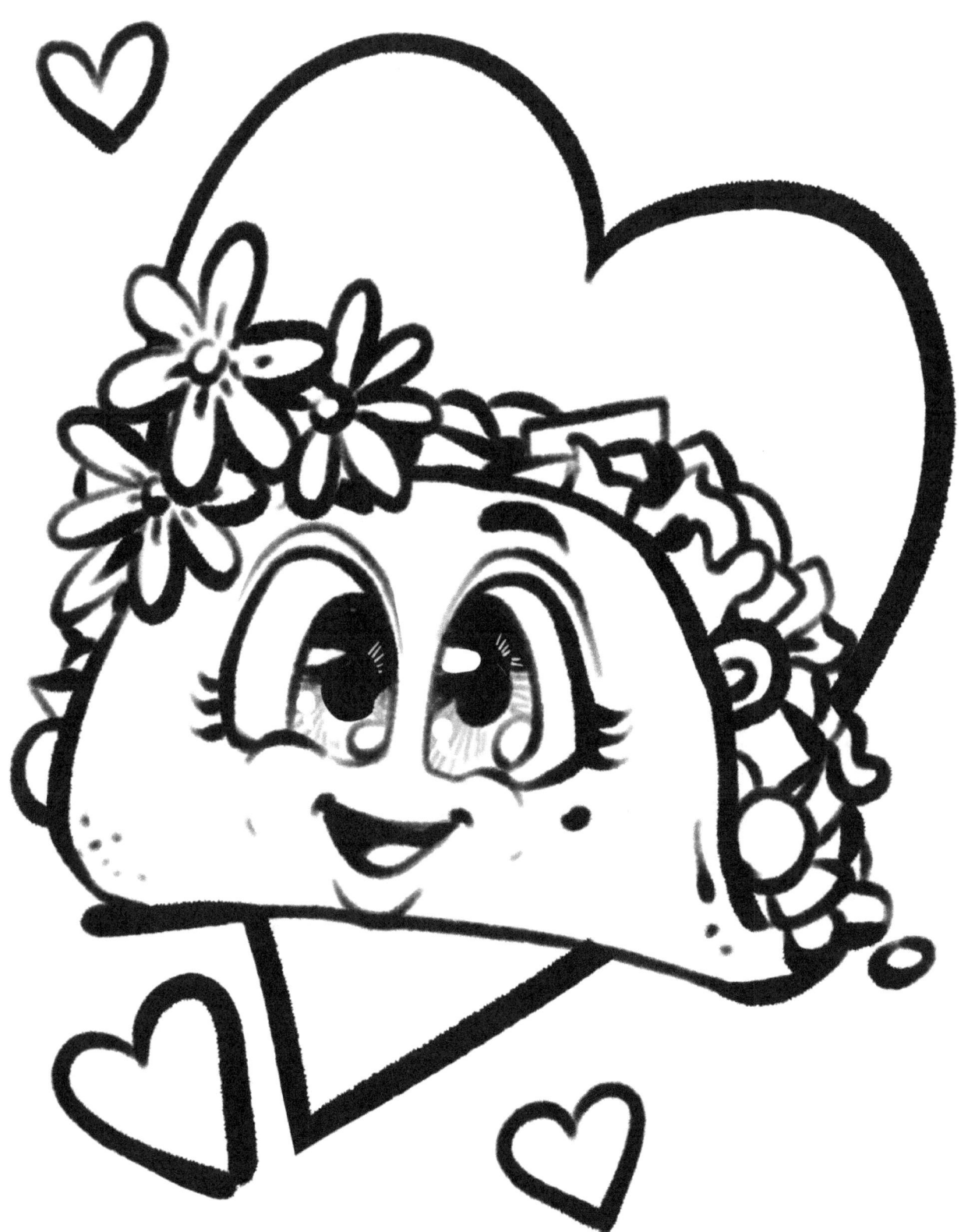

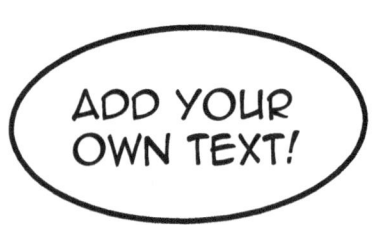
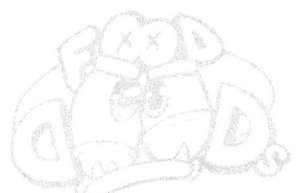

DETAIL LEVEL: LOW

DIFFICULTY: LOW

SPECIES: WAFFLE

NAME:

STRENGTH:

WEAKNESS:

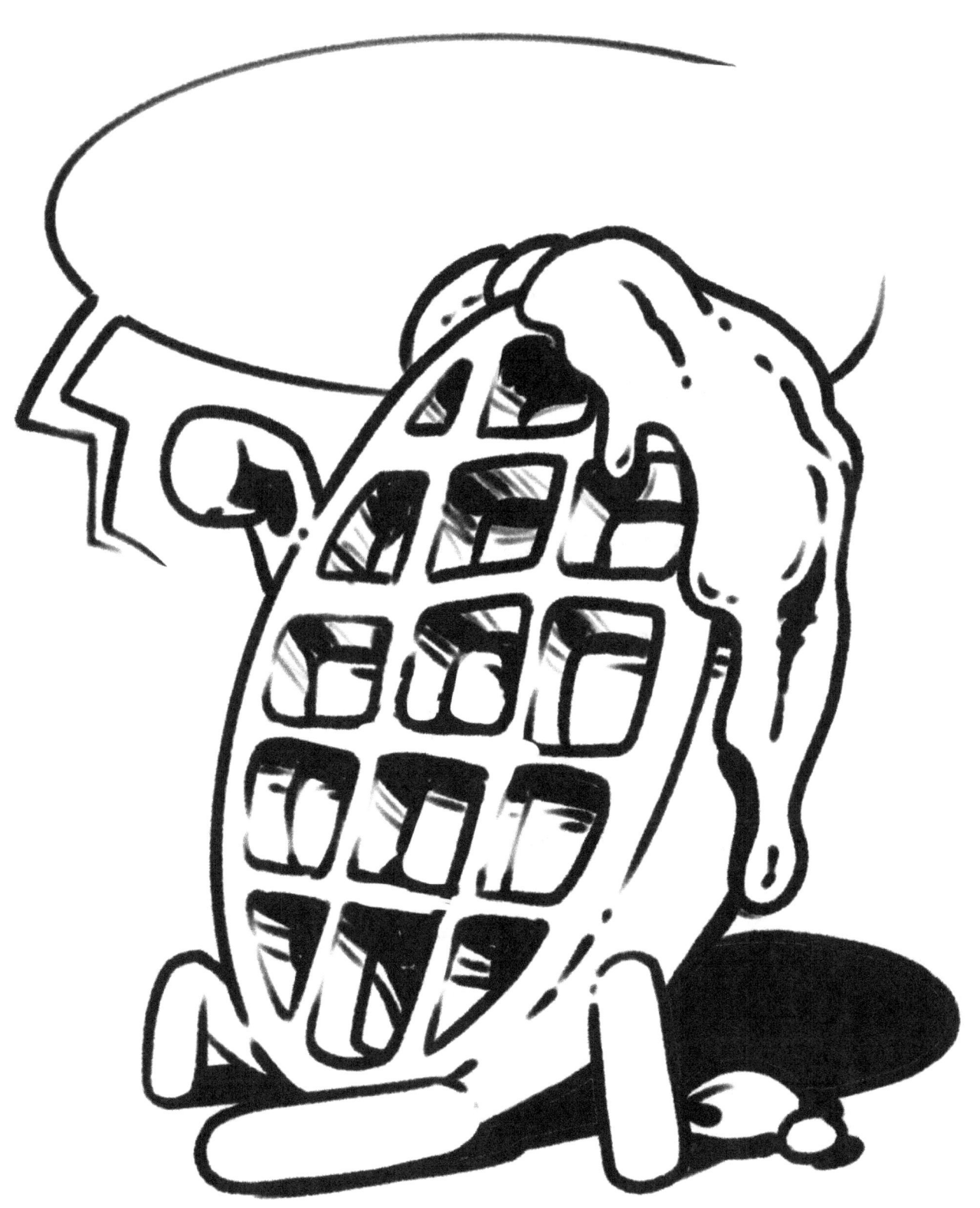

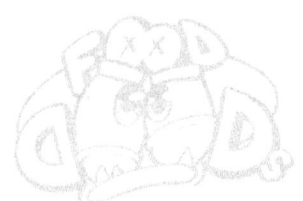

DETAIL LEVEL: LOW

DIFFICULTY: VERY LOW

SPECIES: WATERMELON

NAME:

STRENGTH:

WEAKNESS:

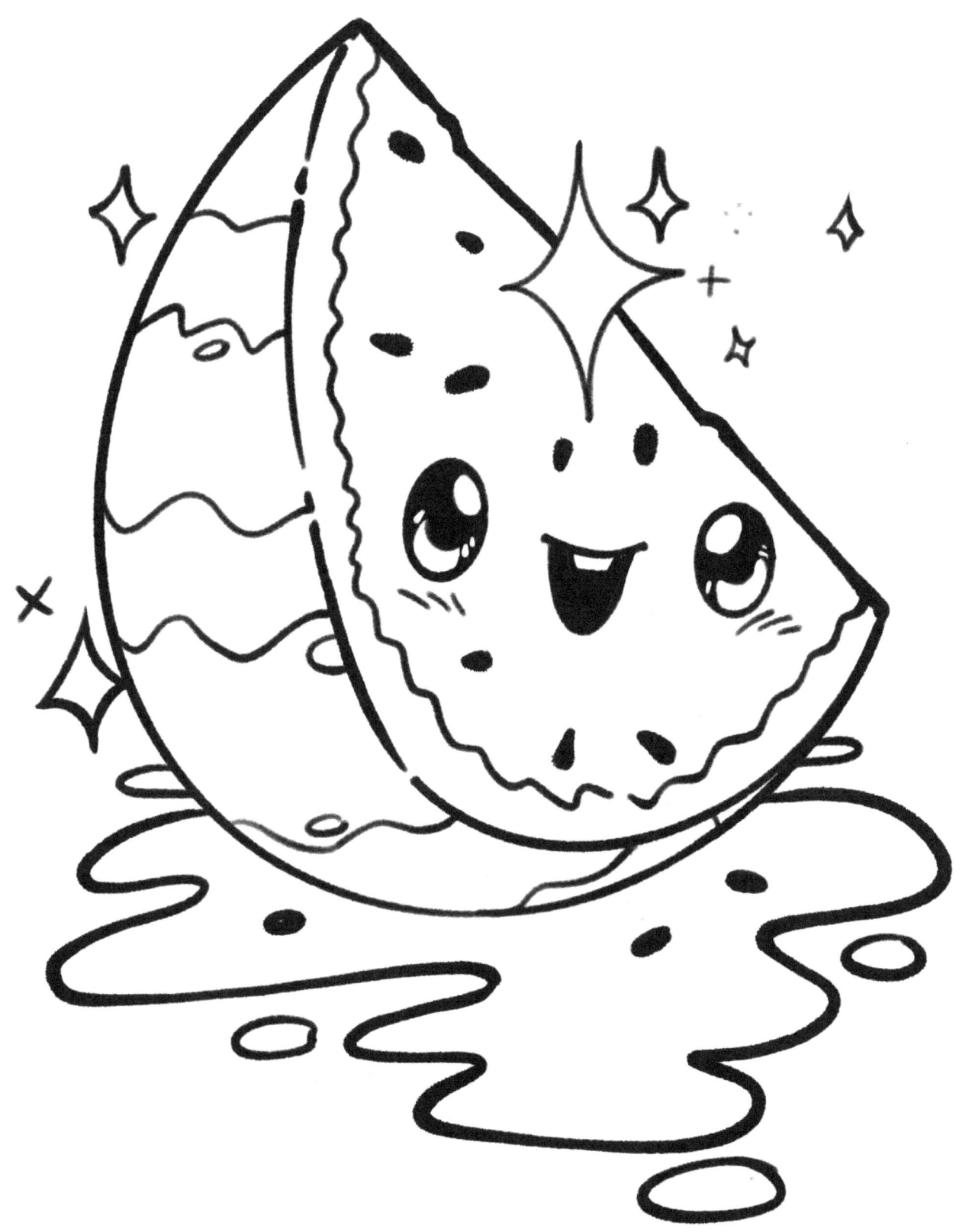

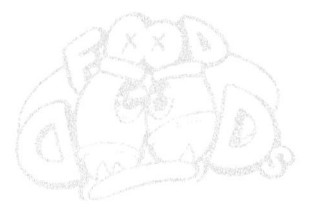

DETAIL LEVEL: HIGH

DIFFICULTY: HIGH

SPECIES: TEA BAGS

NAME:

OPPONENT:

STRENGTH:

WEAKNESS:

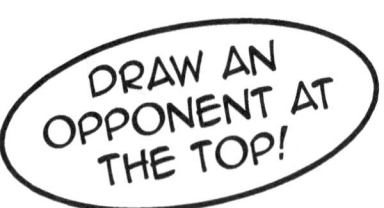

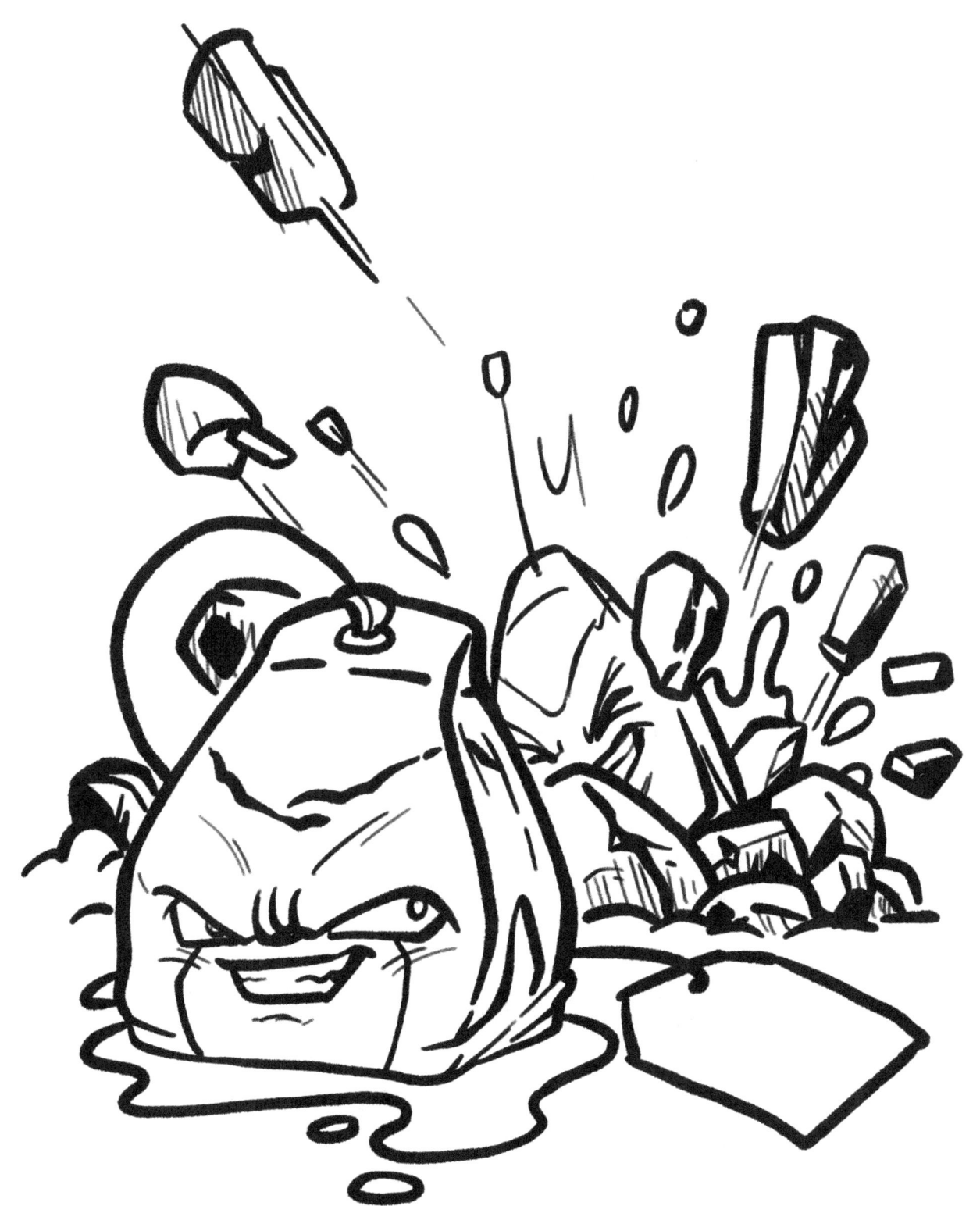

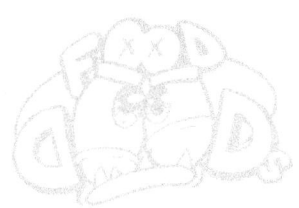

DETAIL LEVEL:

DIFFICULTY:

SPECIES:

NAME:

STRENGTH:

WEAKNESS:

E-MAIL ME YOUR CRAZY MONSTERS AND
IDEAS FOR NEW MONSTERS AT:

TOMISLAVARTZ+BOOK@GMAIL.COM

© Tomislav Artz | tomislav.at | Instagram: jtomislav

IT'S YOUR TURN!

DRAW A MONSTER!

www.ingramcontent.com/pod-product-compliance
Lightning Source LLC
Chambersburg PA
CBHW081459220526
45466CB00008B/2716